SPIRITS ON STONE

THE AGAWA PICTOGRAPHS

Written And Illustrated By

Thor Conway and Julie Conway

HERITAGE DISCOVERIES PUBLICATION #1

Front Cover: The grand shaman Shingwauk.

Published by   Heritage Discoveries
                Suite 108, 763B Foothill Blvd.
                San Luis Obispo, California 93405

Copies of this book can be obtained by sending $8.95 + $1.25 shipping and handling to: Heritage Discoveries, Suite 108, 763B Foothill Blvd., San Luis Obispo, California 93405, or Heritage Discoveries, P.O. Box 269, Echo Bay, Ontario, Canada POSICO.

10 9 8 7 6 5 4
ISBN 1-878094-00-9
Library of Congress Catalog Card Number: 90-82538
Printed in the United States of America

For Amber and Tara, and especially for Fred Pine, SAH-KAH-ODJEW-WAHG-SAH or 'Sun Rising Over The Mountain,' who taught us.

Acknowledgments

The ultimate acknowledgment must go to Shingwaukonce 'The Little White Pine' and several generations of the Pine family, especially Fred Pine and Dan Pine, who have kept their knowledge of this site alive through changing times. Chief Norma Fox, the late Bill Sheshekwin, the late Angus Kapkapshe, and many other native people lead us into an ancient world kept alive through folklore and rituals.

Many individuals in the Ministry Of Natural Resources have contributed to the preservation of this site, of whom we owe special thanks to Cam Clark and Tom Linklater. The late Harry Bussineau, a lifetime resident of the Agawa area, shared his knowledge of Indian history. Mike O'Connor has been a good friend, and has shared in the exploration of Agawa since 1973 when we were young archaeologists falling under the spell of Lake Superior. That summer job turned into a lifetime of exploring Superior's north shore. Selwyn Dewdney became a friend at Agawa. His knowledge and enthusiasm for rock art inspired us.

Jim Morrison worked long hours tracking down information on Myeengun in the Montreal archives. Gustav Nelson shared his extensive knowledge of computer systems, and helped in many ways. Initial site work was done under a Canada Council Explorations grant. The University of Toronto Press kindly gave permission to reprint Selwyn Dewdney's personal discovery of Agawa Rock from the book *Indian Rock Paintings Of The Great Lakes*. Most of all, our understanding and appreciation of the Agawa pictographs comes from our friend Fred Pine. Meegwech Fred, Nimishomis, for sharing your vision with us.

Archives of Ontario photographs appear on pages 3 (#S.13147) and page 13 (#S.7685). National Museums of Canada photographs appear on pages 14 (#36683), 37 (#45815), and 76 (#77894).

Contents

Getting To The Site

The Agawa pictographs are situated on the shore of Lake Superior, about ninety miles north of Sault Ste. Marie, Ontario. It takes a little less than two hours to drive on Highway 17 from Sault Ste. Marie to the site entrance. A large sign marks the turnoff. After a short drive down a gravel road, you will reach a parking area and the trailhead. It takes about ten minutes to walk down a steep trail to the lake.

Allow at least an hour, and more preferably half a day, to enjoy the Agawa pictograph site and surrounding scenic area. The road leading downhill from the parking area goes to one of Lake Superior's treasures—Sinclair Cove. The small beach in Sinclair Cove makes a nice place to eat and relax.

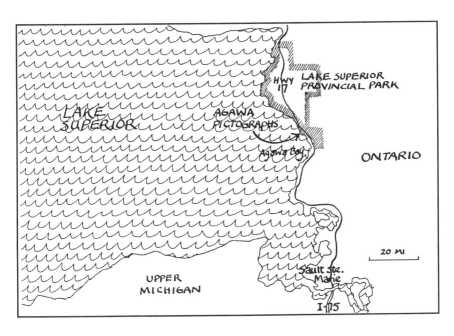

The Agawa pictographs are located near Highway 17 between Sault Ste Marie and Wawa.

Introduction

The first Europeans entering Lake Superior country found a wilderness full of life and clean, fresh water. Ancient white pines increased the height of the cliffs, woodland caribou roamed the forests, and lake trout filled the shoals and bays. Explorer after explorer remarked upon the beauty and natural state of this wondrous land left unchanged by thousands of years of Indian occupation. What greater complement could ever be given to a group of people on this earth? Where else could you find such delicate and respectful interaction between people and nature?

Far back into the mists of time, the Ojibwa Indians first settled along the shoreline of Lake Superior. The native people's ability to preserve the land on which they lived was founded on a subtle understanding of the landscape's forces and powers. The Indians maintained the natural world through respect and ritual observances. The Agawa pictograph site records part of this native religious tradition which combines an understanding of the spiritual and physical landscape.

Agawa Rock stands at the edge of paradise. At least, many travellers experience this feeling when first discovering Agawa Bay. The Indian rock art site is located on the northeast shore of Lake Superior about 90 miles north of Sault Ste. Marie. The entire Agawa area is part of Lake Superior Provincial Park which is administered by the Ministry Of Natural Resources. As a deep bay with several miles of fine sand and gravel beaches, Agawa leads to dense forests and abrupt hills in the interior. The Agawa River mouth served as a focal point for Indian families for thousands of years; and today the pine covered provincial park campgrounds offer the same opportunities for everyone. Agawa presents Ontario's finest natural treasures: a rugged wilderness landscape, wildlife, Indian history, and an unspoiled coastline with easy access from the Trans-Canada highway. A warm, beautiful land in the summer months, Agawa becomes a surreal frost colored landscape in the fall, a bitterly lonely place in the winter, and a wet, insect laden destination in the spring.

We may never know who first discovered Agawa Bay, but Indians have lived there since the end of the last ice age. For thousand of years, the Ojibwa who named and explored the Agawa valley lead peaceful lives. The pictographs are enduring messages from the past, offered to remind us that Lake Superior country is a spiritual landscape. Here you stand at the threshold of many worlds—physical and spiritual, ancient and modern, civilized and wild.

The Ojibwa who made their home at Agawa were a small band of hunters, fishers, and gatherers. Traces of Indian settlements spanning the centuries can be found just below the forest floor. Archaeologists have uncovered flint arrowheads, carefully decorated clay pottery, bone tools, and other intriguing artifacts used long ago. The Agawa band was closely related to the Batchewana band to the south and the Michipicoten group to the north. In the last century, most Indians left Agawa and resettled with their close relatives in the Batchewana Bay area.

The Ojibwa Indians speak an Algonkian language divided into several dialects. The three eastern Lake Superior groups shared a distinct dialect and material culture which differed from the Ojibwa groups resident at Sault Ste. Marie and other bands located west of the Puckasaw at Pic River. The Agawa band of Indians occupied one or two main villages throughout the prehistoric and historical eras. These village sites were located in Sinclair Cove and near the Agawa River mouth. Many smaller hunt camps and family trapping centers are found upriver and on the inland lakes. Coastal fishing sites were commonly used during the spawning seasons.

Very little direct history of the Agawa Indians has survived, but we know that their lands once extended from the mouth of the Montreal River to the Gargantua headland on the coast, and inland to the Agawa Canyon area. For thousands of years, these Indians followed a seasonal cycle based on available food resources. In the spring, they made maple sugar and netted the spring sucker runs. Fishing on Lake Superior in the summer, while collecting edible plants and berries, provided an opportunity for all band members to live together on the coast.

*Across northern Ontario,
Indian families once lived in bark covered
lodges.*

Several Indian bands would gather in the late summer to trade, feast, find marriage partners, and watch shamans perform mysterious rituals. The yearly gatherings of six or more Indian bands enabled religious ideas and rock art concepts to spread rapidly across the landscape.

In the fall, Indians harvested spawning lake trout and whitefish. Single families moved to the interior lakes to fish, trap, and hunt moose and caribou in the winter.

By living in the same place for countless generations, the Lake Superior Indians accumulated a wealth of personal experiences with the surrounding landscape. Their lives were guided by careful rituals which recognized the many subtle interactions between the forces of nature, living off the land, and renewal of resources. Native religion included ancient shamanic practices oriented to a series of sacred sites. Small shrines, isolated vision questing locations, and unusual landscape features associated with mythic heros covered the country.

While Agawa Rock was recognized as a sacred site by the Agawa band, Agawa Rock was more than a local attraction. Unlike many of the more remote pictograph sites in northern Ontario which were used only by local groups of native people, Agawa Rock represented a focal point for several, eastern Lake Superior, Ojibwa bands from Michipicoten to Sault Ste. Marie, and along the upper peninsula of Michigan. The site is the equivalent of a Stonehenge, a one-of-a-kind, regionally important concentration of past spiritual activities. None of the few recorded rock art sites on the north shore of Lake Superior match Agawa in size or importance.

Using This Guide

This guide to the Agawa pictographs is arranged in several sections. The second section, **Six Common Questions About Rock Art**, provides quick answers which will give you a basic understanding about the paintings. The **Discovery And Research** section tells how the site was found and recorded. The spiritual setting is introduced in the chapter **A Sacred Place**. A discussion of the bedrock geology follows in **The Rock**.

The chapter, **An Ancient Art Gallery**, presents a detailed examination of Agawa Rock. Each panel is described in detail. A series of Indian folktales and personal experiences bring the art to life.

The History Of Agawa Rock records the observations of Indians, fur traders, sportsmen, and historians. A short chapter, **Rock Art And The Dating Game**, reviews the meagre evidence used to determine the age of the pictographs.

Several chapters, **Interpreting Rock Art At Agawa, Myeengun's War Party Panel, Understanding The Michipeshu Panel,**and **Secrets Of The Horse And Rider Panel**, include all of the ethnographic interpretations and oral history relating to Agawa Rock. The cultural setting of the Agawa Indians is provided in **Lake Superior Provincial Park Indian History**, while **Other Rock Art Sites On Lake Superior** briefly lists the few known pictograph locations on the greatest of the Great Lakes.

Terms

Panel refers to a distinct part of the cliff where a group of pictographs are clustered or generally inter-related.

Pictograph is a painted example of Indian art. A petroglyph is a carving made into the rock.

Red ochre is a natural mineral also called iron hematite. Red ochre was used as a pigment for the paintings at Agawa. Ochre acts more as a penetrating stain than a surface paint.

Motif refers to a specific symbol such as a canoe motif or a caribou motif.

Safety At The Site

Anyone visiting the Agawa pictograph site must use good judgement and caution. Never underestimate the power of Lake Superior. Even small waves breaking at the site present a danger. Unfortunately, there have been fatalities at Agawa Rock. The sloping area in front of the panels is steep, and very slippery when wet. Wear shoes with good traction, and don't step back too far for photographs.

One calm day several years ago, we stood on the ledge recording a panel. Only small waves, less than two feet high, broke along the base of the ledge. Suddenly, we spotted an enormous wave rolling toward us. We quickly grabbed the cliff as a ten foot tall wave of cold water washed over us. Soaked but safe, we renewed our respect for the powers within nature.

Do's And Don'ts

All archaeological sites are fragile gifts from the past. With rock art, it is best not to touch or moisten the paintings. The Agawa pictographs have endured centuries of harsh weather, pounding waves, and scouring ice. We can help keep the site in its natural state by treating it with respect, as an outdoor art gallery and a native shrine. The site has remained free from vandalism in the past fifty years with one sad exception—the recent, meaningless carvings made by an insensitive person.

Many native people leave gifts at the site. You can join this tradition by placing a small offering of tobacco or coins on the ledge, or by throwing the gifts into the lake. If you observe a broken cigarette, a feather, or some plants on the ledge, leave them as they are recently deposited; and do not photograph the offerings.

Six Common Questions About Rock Art

Several thousand visitors have looked at the Agawa pictographs in the last twenty years. Here are some quick answers to the most common questions asked about the site.

Who Painted The Pictographs?

All of the pictographs at Agawa Rock are the work of Ojibwa Indian shaman artists. The shaman or medicine man handled spiritual matters, conducted rituals, and provided a link between this world and the spirit world. Agawa is an exceptional site because the names of two individuals who painted there are known. One is a 17th century Amikwa band leader named *Myeengun*—'The Wolf.' The well documented Ojibwa leader Shingwauk or 'The White Pine' also painted some of the rock art at Agawa.

How Old Are The Paintings?

None of the art on Agawa Rock is more than three thousand years old, since the water level of Lake Superior rose above the painted areas of the cliff prior to that time. The best guess suggests that most of the visible paintings were completed during the last 500 years.

Why Were These Painted?

The simplest answer is "for a variety of reasons, all spiritual." Most rock art represents the end products of religious experiences such as vision quests, group ceremonies, and acknowledgment of spiritual

Shingwauk the grand shaman of
Lake Superior, and his wife.

assistance. At Agawa, we know that one panel marks success in warfare and another panel shows a vision quest dream. The art is not a direct record of historical events.

What Do The Paintings Mean?

At a handful of sites, some specific panels have been interpreted by the Indian descendants of the medicine men who originally painted the symbols. The Horse and Rider panel preserves a complex record of a vision quest dream and other Ojibwa religious matters. The War Party panel acknowledges spiritual help in victory over the Iroquois raiders.

How Do The Paintings Last So Long?

"You could make a fortune if you knew how to make a house paint last that long today," is a common remark at the site. The pictographs endure the effects of time and waves because they are stains well bonded into the rock wall. Most of the paintings at Agawa have a clear coating of natural "rock varnish" formed by minerals dissolved in rain water seeping down the cliff. After a period of time, the pictographs are no longer directly exposed to the elements.

How Many Paintings Are There?

The current total is 117 pictographs at Agawa Rock. A few were discovered as recently as 1989. Without doubt, dozens more very faint paintings await discovery.

A Special Place
Called Agawa

Agawa Rock stands silently on the shore of Lake Superior. Many individuals have been moved by its power and beauty. All search for answers. From the earliest spiritual people who painted the cliff to more recent tourists and outdoor enthusiasts, Agawa seems to affect its visitors.

Discovery And Research

It is misleading to credit anyone with the discovery of the Agawa pictograph site. The native people along eastern Lake Superior used the site for centuries, and always knew of its existence. You can't discover a site that was never lost. However, one individual brought the Agawa pictographs to national and global attention.

Selwyn Dewdney first learned of Agawa Rock when reading Schoolcraft's work from the 1850's. Selwyn searched for the paintings, and his patience was rewarded in 1958 when he first saw the cliffs at Agawa Bay.

Today, we can easily drive and walk to the site. But Selwyn Dewdney's first journey was more adventuresome. In his book, *Indian Rock Paintings Of The Great Lakes*, he documented the moment of discovery.

> In 1958, however, Mike Kezek's Trail's End Lodge
> at Montreal River was literally the end of the road.
> Thither on a Saturday morning in September four
> of us drove the ninety miles from Sault Ste Marie
> for a rendezvous with Mike and his thirty-five-

foot launch: Gordon Longley, Assistant District Forester, Dave Carter, *Sault Star* feature writer, his wife Ann, and I. In Mike's sturdy lake cruiser we watched the Lake Superior shore go by: the long smooth curve of sand-edged Agawa Bay--calm in an offshore wind--the cluster of rocky islands off the promontory to the north behind which Agawa Rock lay hidden, and to the west the vast sweep of Superior, broken only by the low mass of Montreal Island.

At Agawa even in the calm the water was restless beside the sloping ledge under the sheer cliff and Mike anchored his boat well away. We commandeered a leaky punt from the fish-camp on a nearby island, and paddled ashore with one oar, a piece of plank, and a bailing can. Then, as my diary relates, "I stared. A huge animal with crested back and horned head. There was no mistaking him. And there, a man on a horse--and there four suns--and there, canoes. I felt the shivers coursing my back from nape to tail--the Schoolcraft site! Inscription Rock! My fourteen months' search was over."

Selwyn Dewdney was the father of Canadian rock art studies. A talented person with a wide range of accomplishments including a career in therapeutic art, a successful novel, and scientific studies of native art and religion, Selwyn played a major role in the development of artist Norval Morriseau's career. It is ironic that the pioneer rock art advocate was a catalyst behind Morriseau which ultimately lead to the growth of contemporary Woodland Indian art. Agawa Rock represented one of Selwyn's greatest triumphs. He linked the intriguing accounts preserved by Schoolcraft with this world class pictograph site. Selwyn returned to Agawa many times, perhaps as much for renewal and thought, as for research. The plaque at the edge of the site commemorates Selwyn Dewdney's accomplishments and his final journey to the Agawa shores of Lake Superior.

*Man and nature have marked
Agawa Rock.*

A Sacred Place

Agawa Rock forms a natural cathedral of stone. When visiting the site, remember that this is a sacred location for many native people today. The only true way to gain an understanding of Agawa Rock is through an appreciation of native spirituality.

Visit the site during a quiet time to achieve a sense of place.. Forget the pictographs for a moment and let your senses take over. Lake Superior has moods, feelings, and subtle influences on those who can stand still and let emotional forces take over. The pictograph site location can energize or calm us. The setting certainly leads us away from the 20th century into a more natural world. In some ways, a poet can get closer to the site than a scientist.

The Rock

When geologists visit Agawa Rock, they describe a pink-grey mass of enduring granite with diorite and pegmatite intrusions. However, Indian medicine men view the same cliff in a more animate way. Great vertical cliffs were believed to be 'cut rock'--powerful places where the earth's energies were exposed. In a landscape dominated by glacially rounded rock outcrops, the soaring lakeside cliffs offer dramatic relief. Many cliffs and ledges in northern Ontario have been documented as sacred sites of the Ojibwa. Most of these locations do not show rock art, but such sites are preconditioned for rock art. Rock art sites can be understood as one portion of a larger spiritual landscape.

Visitors to Agawa Rock have commented on the overwhelming vertical beauty of its setting. One friend said, "Even if the rock paintings were not here, almost anyone would be taken in by the natural spirituality of the place." Imagine how much that effect was enhanced to an Indian shaman a few hundred years ago. In those days, all the world was alive. Rocks and trees had souls. Stars controlled events on the earth; and races of elves lived in the forests.

According to the descendants of the Ojibwa medicine men, another natural feature helped determine the suitability of a cliff for rock art.

Over two decades of fieldwork, we could not understand the erratic distribution of pictograph sites across the northern lakes. In some regions, such as the Lake Temagami area, red ochre paintings occur on a large percentage of the seemingly suitable cliffs. It is possible to canoe through the Temagami country and find rock art by checking a likely outcrop. Chances for a pictograph discovery are high in the Temagami area. But the inland lakes and shorelines of the Great Lakes in the Algoma district do not follow this formula. Rock art sites are widely scattered, even though magnificent sheer cliffs are common occurrences.

Why were so many suitable rock canvases ignored by the ancient shaman artists? This puzzle appeared unsolvable until we started to learn more from the Ojibwa medicine people about the cultural settings of pictograph sites. Insights first came in a round-about manner. While collecting the original Indian place names for rivers, lakes, mountains, shrines, old village sites, and travel routes, we found that all pictograph sites once had names. Much of the primary knowledge about rock art locations has been lost through time, but we did recover seventeen original names in northern Ontario.

Many of the specific pictograph site names refer to birds of prey. Each of the named sites is a vertical cliff dropping into a lake. When we pursued this lead, we found that shamans regarded large nesting birds, living atop cliffs, as metaphors for the presence of unseen thunderbirds. Thunderbirds or *Animkeeg* represent tremendous power. Being birds, they travel in the heavens between the earth and the spirit world. Ravens, various hawks, and eagles continue to nest at many rock art sites, as they did in the past. Far up the rock walls, their nests fill small ledges.

A typical rock art site name is *Ka-Gaw-Gee-Wabikong* or 'Raven Rock White Cliff Beside The Water'. The white concept comes from the white wash of bird droppings often seen below active nesting sites. In addition to large birds living at a potential rock art sites, another connection exists. The natural white mineral deposits washed down cliff faces are calcite solutions caused by minerals dissolved in rain water. Shamans view the white calcite deposits as magnified indications of the cliff dwelling thunderbirds' unseen nests. At Agawa, the calcite deposits are prominent.

We do not know the specific site name for Agawa Rock. Schoolcraft reported the general name for the Agawa pictographs as *Mazhenau-Bikiniguning Augawong,* translated as 'Markings On The Rocks At Agawa Bay'. This is a typical, non-specific place-name similar to referring to a store as 'The corner store in Goulais River' rather than a site specific name such as 'Winston's Grocery And Chicken Palace Of Goulais River'.

*While rock art sites were permanent locations for
dealing with the supernatural world, the Ojibwa also built
temporary structures for spiritual communication. This pole
frame is the shaking tent often used by shamans.*
National Museums Of Canada Photo 36683

An Ancient Art Gallery

The Agawa pictograph site is a series of red ochre paintings found four to ten feet above the base of a steep cliff. In the right weather conditions, you can walk to all of the panels. Two panels are situated on the far south end of the cliff. If you do not have a boat or canoe, you can take the back way and walk there from the visitor parking lot. You can also get lost, since no trail exists.

We have studied the Agawa pictograph site for 17 years. In that time, 117 paintings were recorded. Without much doubt, more paintings await discovery at the site. As recently as 1989 another pictograph was found on the cliff (the faint thunderbird on panel I). The clarity of each painting depends upon several variables, including the amount of sunlight, time of day, cloud cover, moisture on the rock surface and individual powers of observation. If you want to search for undocumented paintings, the area between panels I and V offers the greatest promise.

The Agawa pictograph site has been divided into 17 panels. Some of these areas, such as the Myeengun war party group, represent single rock art events where all paintings were done at the same time. Other parts of the site, including panel I and the central *Michipeshu* panel, show superimposed pictographs indicating repeated use over a span of time.

The rock art panels are numbered from north to south (left to right) as you face the cliff. Each pictograph has an individual inventory number. Some pictographs are very difficult to find, but much interesting art is well preserved.

A Fish, Canoes And Caribou (Panels I & II)

The first pictographs at Agawa Rock usually can be viewed even if large waves make the remainder of the site inaccessible. Panel I occurs furthest from the water under the protection of a deep overhang. Bright paintings of a fish and an elongated mythological creature with large ears or horns appear on the wall. A very careful look at the large eared creature reveals a now faint canoe pictograph beneath. A faint thunderbird, located just above the animal and canoe, appears to be associated with the canoe.

A faint, but beautifully rendered, woodland caribou with long antlers stands immortalized on the rock wall a few feet south of panel I. Woodland caribou once lived throughout eastern Lake Superior. Archaeologists have found caribou bones on Indian campsites at Agawa Bay and on Whitefish Island in downtown Sault Ste. Marie. In recent years, caribou have been reintroduced to remote areas of Lake Superior Provincial Park. Like the great flocks of passenger pigeons that once filled the Agawa area, the original woodland caribou were locally hunted to extinction in the past century.

Individual Paintings

◊ A sucker-like fish (1), with whiskers around its mouth, faces north.

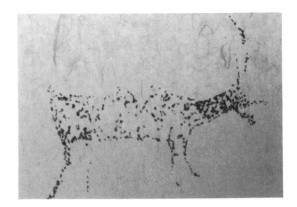

◊ A mythological animal (2) has a pair of large ears, or more likely horns, on its head. Small front and rear legs are also indicated. For the Ojibwa Indians, horns denote exceptional supernatural power.

◊ The horned animal partially covers a faint canoe (3). At least one vertical projection represents an occupant in the canoe.

◊ Like the thunderbird on panel III, this thunderbird (4) is depicted with its wings spread vertically and the head turned to one side. The faint thunderbird flies above the canoe.

◊ A faint woodland caribou (5) shows long, graceful antlers.

Trailing A Caribou

One of the last Agawa band Indians to live in the Agawa Bay area was a remarkable individual named Tauwaub. Stories of Tauwaub's skills survived with Agawa Bay's original pioneers—the Bussineau family. In the early part of this century, Tauwaub worked with the Bussineau family. Once, when camped at Burnt Rock Pool on the Agawa River, Tauwaub told his friends that he sensed his pregnant wife, who was living at Batchewana Bay, was having their baby. Tauwaub walked the time-worn Indian trails to Batchewana, saw his wife and the new baby, and returned by sunrise to continue guiding.

On another occasion, Tauwaub was leading a group of hunters on the trail of *Atik*, a woodland caribou. When asked how far away the animal was from the hunters, Tauwaub simply leaned over and smelled the caribou's tracks. "Fifteen minutes," he answered. According to the published account, the caribou was sighted fifteen minutes later.

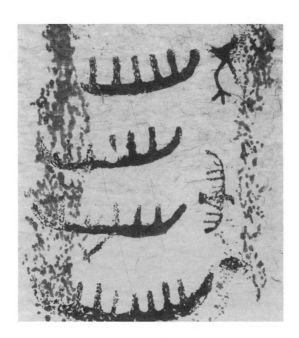

The Wolf's War Party (Panels III & IV)

The vertical group of canoes and animal leaders may be one of the best documented rock art panels in Canada. Unlike so many cryptic rock art groups, the 'Wolf's War Party' paintings can be related directly to a historical event. The panel shows a brigade of Ojibwa canoes, being lead by the totem animals of the Indian clans, during a period of warfare on Lake Superior. The full story of this intriguing panel is told in a later chapter.

Individual Paintings

◊ The Ojibwa warriors' canoes (6 to 9), showing various numbers of occupants, are lined up vertically.

◊ A crane or possibly a sand piper (10), is the main totem animal of many Sault Ste. Marie area Ojibwa families. Painted in profile facing south, the bird leads one canoe. Lichen and calcite deposits now cover part of the crane's head. An eagle (11) is painted in a thunderbird form. The eagle is the main totem of the Mississagi Ojibwa who live on the north shore of Lake Huron near Blind River. Four lines emanate from each wing, and a thick, slightly curved stroke forms the bird's body ending in a fan-shaped tail. The thunderbird's head is turned to one side.

◊ A totem beaver (12) is the ancestral animal of the *Amikwa* Ojibwa who live

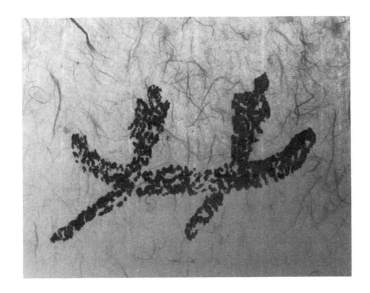

on the shores of Georgian Bay near the French River. The beaver also leads a canoe.

◊ On panel IV, a different canoe motif (13) shows two people and their paddles. Paddles are not illustrated very often in rock art.

My Totem

In 1983, we travelled to Agawa with the noted Ojibwa tribal elder Fred Pine. Mr. Pine, who was born in 1897, is a grandson of the great Lake Superior shaman and medicine man Shingwauk. They share the same family totem animal which is the crane. The shorebird painted on panel III indicates a more distant ancestor of the Pine family who participated in the battle between the Iroquois and the Lake Superior Ojibwa. Most studies have identified the shorebird used by the Garden River area Ojibwa as a clan totem as a crane. Fred Pine disputes this interpretation.

Fred Pine once described his totem.

I got this little bird with the long legs inside me. He walks around very proud. He is a smart bird. He travelled a long ways too. This bird is very quick. That's what I carry. N'Dodem. My totem. Gee-Sheesh-Kinay. Sand piper.

Most native people believe that their totem animal imparts it's qualities and skills to members of the clan.

A Moose, Tracks & Abstract Art (Panels V, VI, & VII)

Panel V has a faint, large pictograph, possibly a canoe which can not always be seen. The moose-like mammal on panel VI is the most easily recognizable painting on this part of Agawa Rock.

Panel VII, which shows considerable evidence of repainting, contains numerous linear abstract pictographs and possible bear tracks. The presence of most of the abstract art on one panel raises more questions still unanswered.

Individual Paintings

◊ A possible large canoe pictograph (14) which is very faint appears to be a wide, thick bodied canoe with several broad lines indicating the paddlers.
◊ A mammal (15), painted in profile facing south, may represent a moose, deer or horse with a short tail and a long muzzle.
◊ A series of faint, abstract paintings (16 to 50) are clustered together on the portion of the cliff below and to the right of the main *Michipeshu* panel. Some motifs, such as 16, 17, and 21, appear to be bear tracks. The short vertical lines, often called tally marks, were used to indicate the passage of time or events. Many of the panel VII pictographs occur in groups of three.

A Boy Is Transformed Into A Bear

Bears play prominent roles in northern Indian society. Numerous folktales document the complex relationship between the Ojibwa and bears. Chief Norma Fox of the Cockburn Island band from Lake Huron once told us about a remarkable transformation.

One time there was a boy who was lazy. From the minute he was born, he wasn't up to it (work). He was just not a mover. When the time came to be an adult, the boy had to go on a vision fast. He went reluctantly. His lodge was set up with a little bit of water, so the boy was set. Even then, the boy was lazy about the fasting. He stayed resting around in the fasting hut for a long time. When his visions became intense, the boy didn't try to save himself. He didn't ask for water. He didn't ask for trees; any of the trees that have fruit or berries for strength, like juniper. Juniper is excellent if you are dying of thirst. The berries somehow kill the tongue to stop your thirst.

The boy didn't do anything to protect himself. His natural laziness caused him to over-fast. The fast is only supposed to last six or seven days. He went way over. Fourteen days.

By now the boy was getting thin. He's so lazy, he didn't want to call out for help. Eventually a vision came to him and told him what to do. The bear was his guiding spirit. The bear said, "You must claw out of this hole." Well I guess the spirit saw how lazy the boy was. The bear tried to convince him to move out of the fasting area so the boy could get some nourishment. This was going on and on. Fourteen; twenty-one; twenty-eight days. It was getting a little too long.

The boy didn't pay attention. Eventually the bear gave the boy claws. The boy's hands developed claws, and his feet now had claws. Even that didn't get him moving, so the boy completely turned into a bear. That's the story and that's what happened.

This story of transformation has a theme common in shamanic lore around the world. The bear represents one of the most powerful forms of alltered state. There are rock paintings elsewhere in northern Ontario showing transformation of people into thunderbirds.

*The central part of Agawa Rock includes the ab-
stract panel, the main Michipeshu panel, and the horse and rider
group.*

Michipeshu And The Snakes
(Panels VIII & IX)

Michipeshu (The Great Cat) is the most famous rock art painting in Canada. *Michipeshu's* turned head enhances the dramatic profile of his body. Lynx-like tufts of fur stick out from his cheeks and dragon-like spines run the length of the back and tail. Even today, native fishermen speak guardedly about the many legends of *Michipeshu*. In many ways, *Michipeshu* is the ultimate metaphor for Lake Superior—powerful, mysterious, and ultimately very dangerous.

Michipeshu lives underwater with the giant serpents like the two depicted here. What are the crescents on the chests of these creatures? Some native people view them as inverted horns of power, but others have identified the crescents as legs.

This panel may have a long history. The present pictographs are painted on a background created by a red ochre wash which obscures previous artwork. There is some evidence that *Michipeshu* too has been repainted at least once. His back legs and tail may have been

extended using a darker ochre pigment. Several sets of faint, finger dragged lines surround the main figures.

Higher up on the cliff, on panel IX, an unique canoe with three tall occupants occurs near an abstract motif.

The Origin Of Underwater Monsters

A story remembered by Fred Pine illustrates the power embodied by underwater creatures.

The animals that live at the bottom of Lake Superior were not created by the Holy Spirit. They don't have hair. Their bodies are covered with fingernail-like scales; and spines run down their backs. A long time ago, gold, silver, and copper minerals were found on the surface of the earth. These scaly animals hoarded the minerals and buried the metal deep beneath the earth.

The Holy Spirit told the medicine men to get rid of the spiny creatures. Those animals ate trees and destroyed the forest. That's when flint was discovered by the Indians. Only flint is sharp enough to pierce their scaly skin. So the Indians, with the help of the spirits and

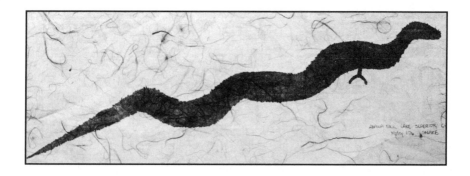

The snakes painted at Agawa have unusual legs or
horns protruding from their chests.

*medicine men, killed off those giant creatures. Only the ones that live
deep under the sea survived.*

Individual Paintings

◊ Four groups of three oblique lines (51 to 53, 58 to 63, and 68 to 70) were
made by dragging ochre-covered fingers across the wall. These marks
record some ancient, uninterpreted activity on this part of the site. The triple
lines appear to be contemporary with the snakes, *Michipeshu*, and the
canoe. They loosely surround these main figures.

◊ The giant serpents (54 and 55) of Ojibwa mythology are called *Chignebikoog*.

◊ Each of the three paintings of *Michipeshu* at Agawa Rock are associated
with canoe pictographs. The grandest *Michipeshu* (56) turns to face us and
display his spiny back and tail.

◊ A faint painting (57) is situated immediately above the large canoe and
another poorly preserved pictograph (67) occurs to the right of *Michipeshu's*
horns.

◊ Two vertical lines (64 & 65) can be found above *Michipehsu's* tail. These
linear abstract paintings are partially covered by the two sets of oblique
finger drags.

◊ *Michipeshu* (66) is the largest pictograph at Agawa Rock. The creature
stands as a silent reminder of Lake Superior's many mysteries, past and
present, that await us along the shoreline.

◊ The light red ochre stain (71) that was washed across the entire panel may
have been done to prepare the rock wall for the dramatic *Michipeshu* group.

◊ The fresh looking, triangular scar (72) on the granite above the canoe

A deep canoe with a high bow and stern is painted on the Michipeshu panel. If we imagine the canoe on the surface of Lake Superior, then Michipeshu is rising out of the water in front.

marks the most recent loss of native art from the Agawa site. According to the published account of a summer visitor, a large slab broke away from this part of the site in the 1870's. Somewhere on the bottom of Lake Superior, a rock is covered with the missing red ochre paintings. Divers have searched for the missing rock, but the severe wave action has hampered their efforts by moving huge pieces of rocks away from the site. Possibly the rock with the paintings may have landed face-down, or the paintings were scoured away by the grinding shore ice. Spalling caused by frost action is unfortunately part of the natural weathering cycle of northern rock art sites.

◊ The isolated panel IX canoe (73) found three feet above the horse and rider panel shows three human figures with tapered bodies.

◊ An abstract painting (74) found even higher up the cliff can only be described as a triangle with a tail.

Wild Men And Giant Snakes

Chief Norma Fox of the Cockburn Island Ojibwa once told of the seven little wild men who paint rock art on cliffs.

*The little wild men often appear on rock
art sites such as this dancing example from Little Missinaibi Lake.*

I never heard of the little wild men wearing clothing. They are a small race of people who talk fast. They do not speak the regular Indian language. The little wild men have a certain language of their own. And nobody understands them.

The pygmies or wild men can capture and kill the Chignebikoog (Giant Snakes), and use the giant serpent's blood to paint on the cliffs. That is why the rock paintings exist today, because of the pygmies and the giant serpents. We call them Puhkudjinnik which means 'Little Wild Men.' The only thing that people remember about them are their eyes. The wild men can harm you by staring.

The cliff paintings are made from the serpent's blood, which proves that if the snake is made of copper or silver, then it can last or endure a very long time. There is a story about the French River colony where the Chignebikgoog (Giant Serpents) live. Lots of those big, long, snakes guard the Great Lakes. At one time, there were giant snakes living at the mouth of the French River on Georgian Bay. The Iroquois were having a war with the Ojibwa; and the French River was the dividing line between the tribes. The Ojibwa asked the Great Spirit to help catch some of the giant serpents. The Ojibwa Indians hired the seven little wild men to do that work. The wild men are the ones who caught the snakes and used their blood to paint on the rocks. There is a rock painting of one of those giant snakes up on the cliff near Killarney.

There is also a legend that an Indian was canoeing on Lake Superior, and suddenly the water became very turbulent. The Indian man was sure he would drown. A big snake was pulling at his canoe, so the Indian stuck his fish spear into the giant serpent's back. When he pulled the spear up, a piece of the snake's flesh was stuck onto the end of the spear. The flesh turned out to be pure copper.

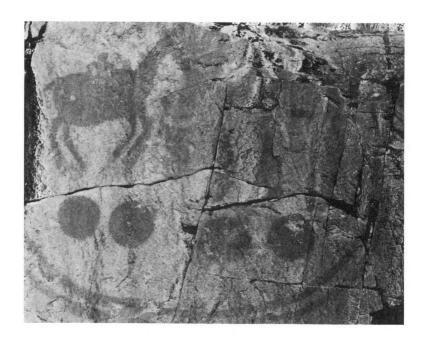

THE HORSE AND RIDER (Panel X)

The horse and rider panel was painted without any doubt after the introduction of horses to North America. For many years, the horse motif provided the only clue to the panel's age (sometime after 1600 A.D.). By the 1980's, research with Ojibwa elders demonstrated that Shingwauk had painted the horse and rider group sometime around 1850. The panel represents a dream from a vision quest. Some of the symbolism refers to Shingwauk's status as a fourth degree member of the *Midewewin* or 'Grand Medicine Society.' More details are presented in a separate chapter of this guide.

Two large concentric circles once enclosed the horse and rider panel. The top arcs of these circles have broken away. In the early 1970's, a few traces of the circles' top arcs remained covered by lichens.

Individual Paintings

◊ The romantic interpretation of these four spheres (75 to 78) as three suns indicating a crossing of Lake Superior in three days was given by Schoolcraft, a 19th century scholar. A more consistent identification explains the spheres as four concentrations of power, relating to the fourth degree of the

Midewewin.

◊ The horse and rider painting (79), or possibly a shaman transforming into a horse, shows a horse characterized by a long tail and hooves. The position of the horse's legs indicates movement.

◊ A pictograph representing an insect (80) with a heart line has been identified as a louse.

◊ The fourth degree *Midewewin* pole (81). Although it resembles a Christian cross, the pole is part of a purely Indian religious movement.

◊ A motif resembling a canoe (82) may be a lunar symbol, related to similar crescent moons found on Ojibwa calendar sticks. These sticks were used to keep accurate notation of time based on a lunar calendar. A single tally mark (83) is painted nearby.

◊ The encircling lines (84 & 85) unify the horse and rider group of pictographs.

◊ Five horizontal lines (86 to 90) appear on the right edge of the panel.

Learning From The Wild Man's Daughter

During a quiet day sitting on the beach at Sinclair Cove, Fred Pine relaxed as he recalled stories passed down in his family about Shingwauk. Shingwauk had several sons. One son, known as *Puhkudjinni*, 'The Wild Man' or 'Wild Elf', was named after the race of tiny fairies who inhabit sacred sites. The Wild Man's daughter raised Fred Pine.

That old woman taught me many things. Most of the knowledge I have about herbs came from her. I would follow her through the bush. "Pick this. Pull out that root," she always told me. That's how I learned.

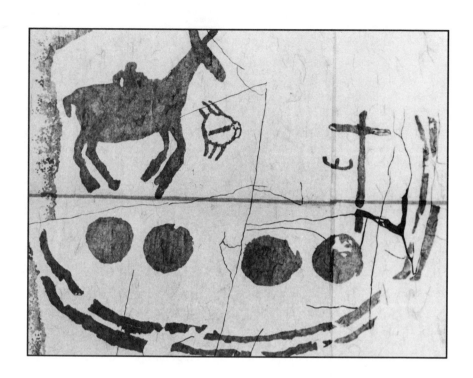

The rice paper copy of the horse and rider panel shows symbols from the Midewewin and Shingwauk's personal dreams. Shingwauk could transform himself into a louse to hide in raven's feathers and fly to distant villages.

She knew her grandfather, old Shingwauk. He could transform himself into any animal. One way he travelled and hid from his enemies was by becoming a louse. When he changed into a louse, nobody could recognize him.

In Shingwauk's time, women hung blankets along tree limbs to air out. Shingwauk would turn into a louse and sit on the blanket. When a raven landed on the tree, Shingwauk would hire him to fly where he needed to travel to do his business. The louse would just crawl onto the raven's feathers and direct the raven. My great-grandfather was a powerful man to be able to change into animals.

Pictographs of horses are very rare in northern Ontario. This example comes from the Mattagami area where a band of Indians named the "Horse People" lived in the 19th century.

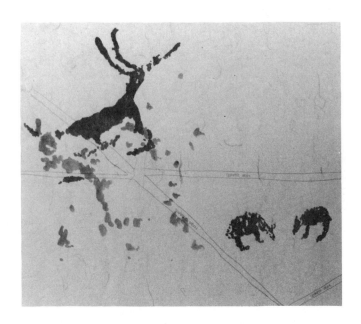

A FAINT PANEL AND THE TWIN BEARS
(Panels XI & XII)

Panel XI is painted just to the right of the five stacked horizontal lines of the horse and rider panel. The top painting of this poorly documented set of three vertically arranged pictographs may be a canoe; the others are very faint.

The twin bears of panel XII show uncommon use of bilateral symmetry in Ojibwa rock art. Carefully painted, the bears were placed inside a triangle naturally formed by thin quartz veins. Some rock art panels incorporate natural features to enhance the presentation. According to legends, quartz veins are filled with power. Quartz veins mark areas on the earth struck by the thunderbirds' lightening bolts.

The Bear Cult

Most northern native groups around the world honored slain bears with a series of ceremonies often referred to as the bear cult. At the Agawa Post, the daughter of the last Hudson's Bay Company fur trader recorded the celebration of a special bear cult ritual. Indians held a ceremony honoring the bear near the Agawa pictographs in the late

1800's. Since pictographs showing bears are rare, it is conceivable that these twin bears were painted at that time.

Individual Paintings

◊ The top painting (91) on panel XI is a canoe with two occupants. The other panel XI pictographs (92 & 93) are too faint to identify.

◊ The first painting (94) on panel XII is difficult to categorize. It appears to be an animal in profile with branching horns and bent front legs.

◊ The tiny twin bears (95 & 96) show the characteristic rounded backs and low-hung heads used by Indian artists to depict these forest dwellers.

◊ A faint pictograph (97) is placed at two intersecting quartz veins to the upper right of the bears. This painting balances the scene, since the horned animal to the left also occurs at intersecting quartz veins.

◊ A single tally mark (98) is clearly visible to the right.

The Last Bear Feast

One freezing winter day, I had an unexplained, urgent feeling that I should talk to Bill Sheshekwin who lived next to Dog Lake on the upper reaches of the Michipicoten River. I had met Bill a few years previously while conducting an archaeological survey of Dog Lake. When I rented a boat from this calm Indian trapper, I asked if he could tell me about Indian life in the area. Bill Sheshekwin told many stories that brought the archaeological sites and landscape to life. Few Indians were left in the Dog Lake area because of the effects of devastating epidemics in the past and few employment opportunities today. Bill obviously retained tribal knowledge that would soon be lost. While rushed that wet summer day, I stood on his decaying dock, listening as I loaded the boat. We shook hands, and I left. I regretted my haste ever since.

Finally that winter morning, I decided that I must salvage an important, almost lost opportunity to interview Bill Sheshekwin. Julie and I drove the long miles from Sault Ste. Marie to Wawa and finally reached Dog Lake.

Bill Sheshekwin was skinning a beaver on his front porch when we arrived. It was as cold inside his house as outside. During our morning together, Bill shared a wealth of native oral history, legends, and local lore with us. A few months later, Bill Sheshekwin was gone forever.

Pictographs showing bears are not common. Some have been located on a lake in the Temagami area.

Bill Sheshekwin displayed the northern native's special respect for the bear. He had participated in many bear feasts; and he knew the rituals necessary to send the bear's spirit off for a happy reincarnation.

Back in the old days, Indians would hang up a bear's head after it was killed. That was done many times here on Dog Lake and up at Lochalsh. We would kill an old bear and have a real feast. There were all sorts of tricks to honor the bear.

In those days, you could go out and kill a bear easily. The bear would be eating blueberries somewhere out there in the bushes. Or sitting there happily. The Indians would wait for the bear to come out of the berry patch, and then they would kill it. Then you take the bear down to the edge of the lake and skin it. Then we had a feast. I can remember doing that too. I was only young, but I went a few times. Normally I would not eat bear if I was paid, but the feast was a special, good time.

The last bear feast on Dog Lake took place over at the narrows. My relatives were picking berries somewhere by the Bailey bridge. There. was very little bush (forest) there in those days, but blueber-

A bear skull hung with respect in a poplar tree near Lac Seul.
National Museums of Canada photo 45815

ries grew there. The Dog Lake Indians went to pick berries whenever they could. Someone took a gun along one day, and he shot a bear. The Indians made their peace with the bear's spirit right in the center of the bridge. Then they dragged the old bear to the north side of the railroad tracks. That is where they built a big fire.

I was there watching the other Indians barbecuing the meat and carefully taking the bones out. They cooked that bear many different ways. I did not want any of it, but you did not dare say anything against the bear, or the old Indians would almost kill you. They thought the bear was something very special. They thought highly of the bear and decorated it with ribbons, gave it tobacco, and hung the bones up in a tree.

THE REINDEER, DRUMMERS & ANOTHER LION (Panels XIII to XV)

The canoe lined up with two deer or caribou is often called Santa and his reindeer for easy reference. Although the canoe painting is unusual, it is not likely Santa's sleigh. The animals resemble woodland caribou. Deer only arrived at the park with the start of logging in the early 1900's.

The drummers recall the mirror imagery of the twin bears. In the old days, each medicine person used a drum to send prayer songs to the spirit world.

The faint profile of *Michipeshu* has spines on its back. There may have been more paintings on panel XV, but only a canoe painting now appears below the *Michipeshu*. At other sites, *Michipeshu* paintings are always associated with various aquatic motifs.

Individual Paintings

◊ The left painting (99) is probably a person in a canoe with a paddle extended over the gunwale. If so, this may be the only Ojibwa pictograph shown in three-quarter perspective.

◊ A deer or woodland caribou (100) is delicately depicted.

◊ A reclining or leaping deer or caribou (101) appears frozen in time.

◊ The two drummers (102 & 103) have a symmetry that reminds us of the Chinese Yin and Yang symbols.

◊ The torso and legs of a partially preserved *Michipeshu* (104) can be seen some days on panel XV.

◊ A simple canoe (105), with two people indicated by vertical lines, is situated below *Michipeshu*.

A Giant Snake At Agawa

Chief Norma Fox has heard several stories about supernatural creatures. The following tale took place at Agawa.

A woman was doing her laundry on the shore of an island near Agawa. It had been a nice, bright sunny day, but all of a sudden the sky clouded up. It did not appear that a storm was coming.

The leaves were not turning over, the wind's direction had not changed, and the amount of moisture in the wind was the same.

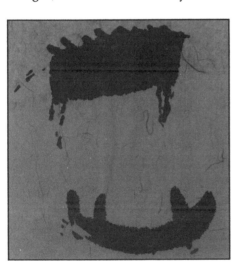

Quickly, the sky darkened more, and great flashes of lightening appeared. Not far away from the woman, the waters of Lake Superior swirled. She recalled seeing a silvery form being carried into the sky by a giant thunderbird.

Thunderers are always protecting Indian people by hunting the giant serpents.

MICHIPESHU WATER GROUP & THE TURTLE (Panels XVI & XVII)

The last panels at Agawa make the hike through the tangled forest worthwhile. Arriving on this steep ledge, you will find a well preserved *Michipeshu* with forward sweeping horns accompanied by a fish and a canoe. The group appears frozen in time. Like the other *Michipeshu* panels, this one has thematic unity. Each of the paintings relates to the waters of Lake Superior with the fish representing creatures that dwell totally underwater. *Michipeshu* is capable of living in the depths or moving onto the shoreline, while the canoe represents activity on the surface of the lake.

Turtle The Messenger

Fred Pine recalled a story about turtle acting as a messenger.

The Indians on Lake Superior could send messages across the lake to the south shore to get help. They did not have any telephones. How did they get those messages over there? The spiritual people used the animals that lived here. Medicine men employed many animals for their work. Turtle was the leader of the animals. He could travel on

the land and in the water. Every place.

Medicine men used turtle many times. They studied him. Look around in the sand, dig around there, and you will find the little turtles. Just hatched. They studied the turtles and figured out how far the turtle travelled. He's been around. The Indians figured turtle had been south someplace. That is how the Indians learned where the rivers ran. The land is tipped over, and the water runs down to the ocean. First turtle travelled that route, then he told the Indians.

Individual Paintings

◊ A faint painting (106) is part of the water group.

◊ A fish in profile (107) and a deep canoe (108) are well preserved on panel XVI.

◊ The last *Michipeshu* (109) on Agawa Rock is unique with his sweeping horns.

◊ A pigment daub (110) is found below the fish; and a faint line (111) occurs below *Michipeshu.*

◊ A turtle (112) leaves a red ochre trail which may be a clue to interpreting the painting.

◊ A daub of red ochre pigment (113) is present below the turtle. Because three of the pictographs on panel XVI show daubs of pigment or small lines

Two mammals, divided by a natural fissure, face each other. A faint painting and a canoe motif occur below.

below major motifs, we believe the daubs and lines are intentionally done.
◊ Two simplified mammals face right (114) and left (115). They are lined up along a natural vertical fissure. A faint painting (116) occurs below the left mammal.
◊ A two occupant canoe (117) was placed below the right animal.

The Celestial Turtle

The painting of the turtle and his trail is unique to Agawa. Fortunately, we can interpret the motif by listening to an Ojibwa creation legend collected years ago on Georgian Bay. For the Indians, every star in the sky has a story which explains its origin and its effect on earthly events. The Milky Way, that great trail of distant stars across the vault of the night sky, was regarded as *Chibay-Meekaun* 'The Path Of The Souls' by the Ojibwa. When a person died, the soul followed the path westward to the land of the souls. Just as the Milky Way has many branches off its path, so the soul encountered false trails along its journey.

An ancient legend tells us how the turtle created the Path Of The

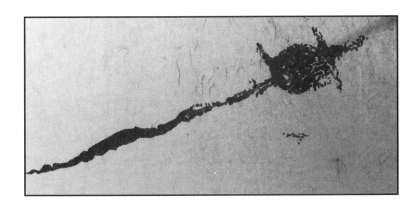

*The turtle and its trail through the mud refer to
an ancient Ojibwa legend about the origin of the stars.*

Souls by flinging mud into the sky from the newly formed earth. Each bit of mud became one of the millions of stars. His work being done, the turtle ascended the path and travelled slowly across the sky. The slow, shifting movement of the Milky Way, as it turns from one direction to another, mimics the turtle's naturally slow progress in the mud and sand.

Legends, so carefully preserved by tribal story tellers, have put the breath of life into rock art images. As Fred Pine once explained,

When I see one of those marks, I know what it is right away. But there's more meaning to it. It's like shorthand. You have to dream about it. It's an effort on your soul by the spirits.

In 1973, I was excavating the Agawa Hudson's Bay Company post archaeological site near the mouth of the Agawa River. During a break from the dig on a hot July afternoon, my friend Mike and I walked along the beach enjoying the cooler air. A short distance away, in the shimmer of bleached logs and grey gravel, we noticed an unusual visitor. As we came closer, we encountered a weathered, rugged shell from which protruded a cold-eyed, reptilian head. Snapping turtles don't usually live in Lake Superior, but this elder of the turtle clan had obviously made the lake a home for many generations. We faced a turtle huge, ancient, and as mysterious as the painting that may have

Turtle often acted as a messenger to the spirits, especially in the shaking tent ceremony. This turtle was painted on Little Missinaibi Lake.

been inspired by his forbearers.

Although I never again saw a snapping turtle in the cold lake, the painted image and this once-in-a-lifetime visitor left me with special images from the past and an inspiration to think more deeply about the magic that awaits us at Agawa Bay.

The History Of Agawa Rock

The early history of the Agawa pictograph site disappears into the mists of time. Fortunately, with the survival of native culture in northern Ontario, we are left with a rich, living legacy.

By the late 19th century, another source became available for learning more about Agawa. Seasonal groups of sports fishermen and hunters were guided along the Lake Superior coast by local Ojibwa residents. Some of the visitors wrote of their experiences in travel books. One author complained of the slow pace of his canoe journey. Every time a cloud larger than a handkerchief appeared in the sky, his Indian guide pulled ashore to make camp. Eager to catch large fish and explore at a faster pace, the visitor wanted to ignore the centuries of accumulated experience carried by his companion. Local residents knew about the sudden winds that could change a calm Lake Superior into deadly sea. These winds were often preceded by a few, meek puffs of cloud.

Many travellers have passed Agawa Bay and the pictograph site, but only a few left us accounts of its daily life or natural attractions. In the spring of 1879, a newspaper, called *Forest And Stream/Rod And Gun The Sportsman's Journal*, published the details of a journey made the previous summer. The three page article, published on Thursday May 22 in volume 12, number 10, recorded the anonymous author's comments under the heading "The Agawa".

After sailing up the coast from Sault Ste. Marie, he found this remarkable place.

We were at last at the Agawa. It had been thought of
for a year or two before opportunity offered for a
visit. I had heard much of it. Some of my friends had
gone in canoes up to the falls, eight or ten miles
from the mouth, and had given glowing accounts of
the fishing and the scenery. I found it a cold stream,
with clear water, and with trout in every pool and
upon every rapid.

Their success seemed ensured. And we later learn that the party
caught "immense strings" of trout, weighing between one half pound
and three and a half pounds, on the first two miles of the Agawa River.

After the mandatory fish stories, the 19th century correspondent
presents us with a glimpse of the pictographs.

We passed slowly along the Agawa Island rocks, saw
the paintings upon them, done probably centuries
ago - although some of them, judging from the
picture of a horse there, must have been painted
within two centuries - Now alas! from the action of
the elements, obliterated. Last year, when I passed
there, I found the frost had scaled great pieces off
the rocks, and the best of the pictures are gone
forever. There are yet left some of the coarser ones
- a caribou, a bear, and some others of animals.

An earlier fur trader named Daniel Harmon recorded a more
indirect reference to the site in his *Journal Of Voyages And Travels
In The Interior Of North America*. Harmon noted many prominent
locations on his trip west in 1800. Travelling along the north shore
of Lake Superior, from Sault Ste. Marie to Michipicoten, Daniel Harmon commented on the Agawa pictographs. On June 1st, 1800 A.D. ,
a brigade of thirty-five canoes left the Soo. By June 4th, he had
reached Batchawana Bay which can be identified from the reference
of meeting St. Germain, the head of the nearby Northwest Company
post. A diary notation for June 5th contains a passing reference to the
Agawa pictograph site.

Although the swells in the Lake are very high, we
have made good progress, during the whole day. We
are encamped near a large rock, on which the Na-

In the last century, Great Lakes travellers used sail boats to reach isolated parts of Lake Superior.

tives, as they pass this way, leave an arrow or two, or some other article of little value to appease the Devil, or *Muchimunatoo* as they call him, and prevent him from doing them harm.

The identification of the large rock as the Agawa pictograph site is based on several clues, including the distance Harmon's party canoed each day. From his journal, it is apparent that Harmon travelled between thirty and forty miles daily. He paddled one day to travel from the Northwest Company post at Batchewana to the campsite near Agawa Rock. The following day, June 8th, Harmon mentioned passing several islands. These are the Lizard Islands and Leach Island. By the morning of June 9th, he had passed the Northwest Company post at the mouth of the Michipicoten River near present day Wawa, Ontario.

Another clue for identifying the large rock as Agawa Rock comes from the surviving oral traditions of the Ojibwa fishermen. Indians continue to regard the massive cliffs of Agawa Rock as a location

The Devil's Armchair is a large rock used by Indian fishermen and travellers to acknowledge the forces of Lake Superior. According to legend, the rock was formed when Nanabush sat there long ago.

connected to powerful spirits. Only two such spirit rocks, the Agawa pictographs and the Devil's Armchair, are identified along the Lake Superior coastline between Batchewana and Michipicoten. The Devil's Armchair is located off of Gargantua Point well north of the islands mentioned by Harmon.

Being near a voyageur encampment, the Agawa pictograph site fits Harmon's description. Sinclair Cove, which is situated just north of Agawa Rock, holds evidence of voyageur encampments. Archaeologists found extensive evidence of fur trade era camps there, as well as the remains of previous Indian settlements. Most canoe brigades, travelling north, made the risky traverse directly across Agawa Bay by starting at the mouth of the Montreal River, landing at Agawa Rock and the shelter of Sinclair Cove.

Today few people remember the origin of the placename for Sinclair Cove. The late Harry Bussineau, who grew up at Agawa Bay, explained how Sinclair Cove was a misunderstood name. The original name was Saint Clair's cove. Whether St. Clair was a voyageur, an early French trader, or a name left by a missionary remains unknown.

The Indians of the upper Great Lakes regarded many dramatic rock formations as the homes of spirit forces. Almost all pictograph sites fall into a larger group of sacred sites which served as shrines. The Ojibwa recognize a string of spirit-inhabited rocks along the north shore of Lake Superior from Old Grandmother Frog Rock, at the entrance of Whitefish Bay, to a Nanabush Rock located a few miles west of the Michipicoten River. Traditionally, offerings have been left at each site.

The Indians told Daniel Harmon that the Agawa cliff was the home of *Muchi-manidoo*. This term translates as 'fearsome spirit'. At Agawa Rock, the most likely candidate for this title is the great guardian of the underwater realm, *Michipeshu*. The Ojibwa believed this lion-like mythological animal was the controlling spirit of Lake Superior. In addition to the three *Michipeshu* rock art panels at Agawa, *Michipeshu* is the subject of many legends throughout the northern Lake Huron and Lake Superior areas. Unusual rock formations resembling *Michipeshu* found near Thunder Bay and Thessalon, Ontario are mentioned in native folklore. Offerings were routinely left at these rocks as an insurance policies for safe travel on the Great Lakes.

Daniel Harmon also recorded arrows left by the Indians at Agawa Rock. Firing projectiles at rock art sites was a wide-spread practice in the northern Woodlands. Also, modern evidence for this practice is evident at some sites. A pictograph cave in the upper peninsula of Michigan has been studied by archaeologists. By digging into the cave floor below the paintings, the archaeologists found the shattered tips of flint arrows or spear points. Nearby, the broken point bases were uncovered from the same stone weapons . After excavation, the bases were refitted to the tips. Judging from the type of artifacts recovered, Indians shot arrows or threw spears at this pictograph site in Michigan nearly two thousand years ago. From this archaeological excavation, we now know that the practice of leaving offerings from a distance is well rooted in antiquity.

When the Scottish fur trader Alexander MacKenzie paddled through northern Minnesota, he found Indian arrows sticking out of a crevice at a rock art cliff. In recent times, anthropologists working with the

*A stone axe, flint projectile points, and a
drill found near Chapleau, Ontario are typical northern
Indian tools. We now know that some projectiles were
used to carry offerings to rock art sites.*

Cree hunters in northern Manitoba have observed Indians firing
their rifles at a rock formation containing pictographs.

It's tempting to view this behavior as an example of hunting magic, since
painted animals are found at so many rock art sites. This conclusion would
seem logical, but for the important observations made by the French
adventurer Chevalier De Troyes in the late 1600's. While De Troyes
was travelling along the upper Ottawa River, on the present-day
border between Ontario and Quebec, the Indians in his party shot
arrows at a rock known today as the Ouiseau Rock pictograph site.
Also, De Troyes' journal suggests that the Indians were afraid of the
spirit powers in the rock, and would not go too close. So, they left
offerings by tying tobacco to the tips of the arrows and firing the
arrows at the rock. De Troyes brief notation provides an explanation
for the other accounts.

Rock Art And The Dating Game

How old are the pictographs? For many years, this was an unanswerable question. Two very different sources have provided some answers to the dating game. One source relies upon the scientific side of archaeological research; the knowledge preserved by tribal elders is the second source. Several scientific tests have succeeded in giving us new dating information; other attempts, such as measuring lichen growth rates, have lead nowhere.

Archaeologists regularly use the carbon-14 technique to date Indian sites in Ontario. Not far from Agawa Rock, a hearth in an Indian settlement was dated to 300 A.D. using the radio-carbon technique. Could this method work for rock art? In recent years, carbon dating has been refined. Only a minute amount of an organic substance is required for study, whereas in the early days of C-14 technology, a larger sample of organic material was needed to obtain an accurate date. We now know from native Indian sources that the materials used to bind the red ochre to the rock surface were organic materials including melted animal fats and fish glues. When tiny samples of the rock paintings were analyzed, only the mineral pigments were detectable. The organic paint elements, such as the grease or glue, had weathered away. This was disappointing, because it is possible to date this organic material.

However, scientists from The Canadian Conservation Institute in Ottawa discovered, upon close examination, important new data about pictographs. Researchers took small pigment samples from rock paint-

Fred Pine learned the practical skills, lifeways, and folklore that characterize the Ojibwa Indians of the upper Great Lakes.

ings from several sites across Canada, including Agawa Rock. These samples were studied in cross-section under the immense magnification of an electron microscope. For the first time, we learned that the pigment usually occurs beneath a clear layer of water deposited minerals, a sort of 'rock varnish'. This told us that the pictographs had the possibility of being hundreds, if not thousands, of years old. Since the paintings were covered with a translucent, or in some cases opaque, wash of rain-leached minerals, the direct weathering process stopped after awhile. The whitish to clear deposits were formed by minerals dissolved by rainwater which washed down the rock face.

The next discovery from this study was the presence of multiple layers of pigment and mineral deposits. There were examples of the granite cliff wall having multiple mineral layers such as (1) the transparent top mineral layer, (2) the pigment from the currently visible painting, (3) another mineral layer, (4) pigment from an

The now destroyed Horwood Lake pictographs offered dating clues based on overpainting.

older painting no longer visible, (5) another mineral layer, (6) more ancient, mineral layers and finally (7) bedrock. While exact dates could not be determined from this work, we now knew that many of these sites had much greater antiquity than ever suspected.

Another often suggested approach to rock art dating is based upon the different styles of the paintings. Is there an evolution of styles from natural representations to more abstract or linear forms? Such hypotheses have been tested around the world with very mixed reviews. Ojibwa rock art does not have enough superimposed paintings to set up an accurate, style-based chronology.

Recent ethnographic research done with Ojibwa Indian medicine men knowledgeable about rock art has placed some of the pictographs within a chronological context. But more importantly, we learned that different styles of pictographs were used by different types of medicine men at the same point in time at Ojibwa sites. We know that much of the vision quest art depicts spirit helpers in the form of animals. However, the Wabeno medicine men often painted rock art in very abstract styles, sometimes depicting the passage of time with rows of tally marks.

*Red ochre canoes from the French
River have been identified by Nipissing Indians as
rock art done against the Iroquois invaders. The
oral history associated with this panel dates it to
the mid-1600's.*

Interpreting Rock Art At Agawa

When you visit an Indian rock art site and ask, "What do these paintings mean?", you are responding for an important reason. Pictographs are messages from the past. The Indian medicine men who painted these intriguing symbols on ancient rock walls chose to make enduring statements. This practice is not so different from our culture's use of stone monuments and other markers created to endure the centuries.

We were able to learn more about the cultural background for the Agawa rock art site, by working extensively with two Garden River band, Ojibwa medicine people: Dan Pine Sr., born in 1900, and Fred Pine, born in 1897. Both tribal elders live on the Garden River Ojibwa Reserve, near Sault Ste. Marie, Ontario. Dan Pine is widely recognized as an Ojibwa religious leader. He is the grandson of Shingwaukonce (Little White Pine). Fred Pine, the oldest person on the Garden River Indian Reserve, is a great-grandson of Shingwaukonce. Fred Pine is a very traditional Ojibwa who as a child, was selected for individual instruction in shamanism. He is one of the last living Ojibwa men, in the Sault Ste. Marie area, to have gone on a vision quest.

Both elders are intimately acquainted with shamanic knowledge and symbolism associated with *Midewewin*, *Djiski-innini* (*Jessakid*), and other Ojibwa religious-belief systems. As direct descendants of the 19th century grand shaman, Shingwaukonce, these men are very knowledgeable about rock art from the Pine family tradition, and

*Dan Pine Sr.
has shared his heritage and
healing skills with many
people.*

from their special training in shamanism.

Additional cultural information for the Agawa pictographs was provided by several Agawa band members, including the late Mr. Angus Kakapshe. Local native people also documented native rituals which have taken place at the Agawa pictograph site in recent years. Only by developing trusting relationships with Ojibwa shamans, will the oral history about rock art become available. It has been easier to colect ethnographic material relating to sorcery than to rock art. Although malevolent shamanism is an uncomfortable topic for the Ojibwa elders, rock art ethnography is considered even more sensitive.

You can burn a bible, but you can't burn this rock. The rock guides. When I see one of those marks, I know what it is right away. But there's more meaning to it. You have to dream about it. Pictographs are She-Twa-Muzzin-Abee-Egun.

Some rock art has disappeared lately. Indians covered the rock up with six or seven inches of sand and gravel. They held meetings and studied there.

One mark on the rocks is a tremendous amount of meaning. It's like shorthand. If one of the painted animals bites you, don't follow the road. Biting is a saying. It's an effort on your soul by the spirits. You become uncontrolled.

Time is running out. Within the decade, there may be no shamans left with this invaluable knowledge.

Myeengun's War Party Panel

The paintings on panel III are the oldest of the few well dated rock paintings in Ontario. Many sources of information contributed to an understanding of the origins of this intriguing panel.

It all began with Indian warfare.

The long years of the 1600's were a time of tremendous change for the Ojibwa people of Lake Huron and Lake Superior. The demand for furs to trade for European commodities in the lower Great Lakes lead to wide-spread warfare breaking out among neighboring native groups. Eventually the Huron and related farmers in southern Ontario were reduced to a refugee population fleeing for their lives to the northern lakes. The Iroquois tribes, originally living in present-day New York state, followed the Indian travel routes into northern Ontario in a quest for more animal pelts.

Iroquois attacks caused a disharmony that reached Algonkians at the community level. Numerous killings, burning of villages, the theft of furs, and related violence brought a need for sorcery rituals to the group level. This may explain the permanence given to some sorcery rituals through the practice of rock art.

Ojibwa medicine people practiced two types of sorcery rituals involving rock art and the Iroquois. The first type ended with the creation of pictograph panels painted by the Ojibwa after successful battles. These panels usually contain several motifs, often showing the Ojibwa participants in groups of canoes, led by the totem animals of the war leaders.

The second ritual, which summoned spiritual help from sinister forces, took place prior to expected warfare. The sites identified with these rituals display single canoes painted on individual panels. The canoe paintings served as public notices of completed rituals, and as a permanent warnings to the Iroquois raiders.

The best example of commemorative ritual art is preserved at the Agawa pictograph site on Lake Superior. There are 19th and 20th century ethnographic sources that enable us to interpret the panel attributed to a shaman named Myeengun, The Wolf.

While working as an Indian agent at Sault Ste. Marie, Henry Schoolcraft made extensive research into Ojibwa culture. He was thorough in his study of native American art. The six volume set, *Intellectual Capacity And Character Of The Indian Race*, contains numerous Ojibwa drawings from *Midewewin* scrolls and some rock art sites. Volume 1 of Schoolcraft's work provides information on two related rock art sites on Lake Superior which are associated with early warfare between the Ojibwa and the Iroquois raiders. One Indian, named Myeengun, was responsible for the pictographs at these sites.

Who was Myeengun? Shingwaukonce supplied a story as well as drawings of Myeengun's pictographs to Schoolcraft in the 1840's.

> Myeengun, or the Wolf of the Mermaid, (or rather,
> as the language has it, Merman totem), who was
> skilled in the Meda, and was invested by the opinion
> of his people, with a character of much skill and
> secret power, He practised the arts and ceremonies
> of the Meda, and made cheekwondum. By these
> means he acquired influence, and raised a war party
> which crossed Lake Superior in canoes. The expedi-
> tion was not barren in other respects of success,
> but this exploit was considered as a direct evidence
> of the influence of his gods, and it gave him so much
> credit, that he determined to perpetuate the mem-
> ory of it, by a Muz-zin-a-bik-on. He made two in-
> scriptions, one on the south, and the other on the
> north shores of the lake. Both were on the precipi-
> tous faces of rocks. Copies of both are presented
> (Schoolcraft, 1851-1857: 406).

While Schoolcraft's writing is somewhat formal, he does convey a relationship between the Myeengun panel and success in warfare. A search through the French and missionary records did not reveal a Myeengun who lived in the Lake Superior area, prior to the 19th century. However, there is evidence of a leader, named Myeengun, who signed the 1701 treaty of peace in Montreal. There, 'chef mahingan' signed with the mark of a beaver. Chef or Chief Myeengun was identified as an *Amikwa* (Beaver) Indian. The *Amikwa* people lived at the northeast end of Lake Huron, in the vicinity of the French and Whitefish Rivers.

The *Amikwa* chief, named Myeengun (Wolf), was important enough to represent his people at the 1701 treaty, which partially ended the conflicts between the Ojibwa and the Iroquois. This association of the *Amikwa* leader, Myeengun with warfare coincides with the account given to Schoolcraft. The temporal setting is also correct. More recently, Garden River band elder, Fred Pine, supplied the following oral history about Myeengun. This interview, which took place in 1983 at the Agawa pictograph site, was made during an extensive discussion on rock art traditions. There is no doubt that Fred Pine's Myeengun story originated with Shingwaukonce and had been handed down within the Pine family.

Myeengun was a medicine man too. Shingwauk and Myeengun made peace with the Iroquois somewhere around Wasaksing 'Beaver Stick Place' (Parry Sound, Georgian Bay on Lake Huron). The Ojibwa tribes went down there in their canoes. That's where they gathered, the Iroquois and Ojibwa, to make their final peace after fighting for years. That's where their lands would separate.

"It's no use killing one another," Myeengun said. "You want to live and we want to live too. So we want this land here (upper Great Lakes). You got Quebec. You got all kinds of water there. You got fresh water. You got everything you want. What do you want to come up here for? What do you want from us?"

People went down to Parry Sound in canoes to make peace. That's where they talked to Myeengun. He was the head man. He was the Ojibwa leader. So he agreed to that. He made peace. They lit their pipes and smoked together.

Around that time, Myeengun said to the other tribes, "We might be

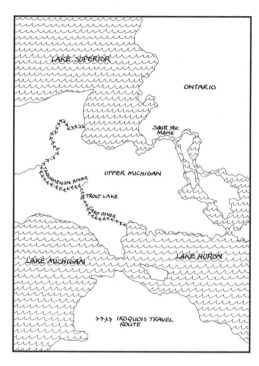

The Iroquois travelled into Lake Superior by an old canoe route.

invaded again. This country of ours will be invaded. There are people elsewhere."

In May 1985, F. Pine contributed the following additional history about Myeengun.

Myeengun came from the French River area. He was a great medicine man. Myeengun was with the first people that were attached by the Naudoweg (Iroquois). They got caught on an island at the mouth of Wemitigosh Zibi (French River) called Maymeissinahkwug, or 'Heavy Bush Island'. Indians went out there to get cedar bark and birch bark.

Myeengun escaped from there, but many people got killed, even women and children. That's when the war between the Ojibwa and Iroquois started. People gathered up for protection. Myeengun and others came over to Lake Superior.

The Ojibwa were waiting in ambush for the Naudoweg (Iroquois) near Sault Ste. Marie. The Naudoweg came up through Michigan by the Carp River and Trout Lake. That's when they fought off of Agawa. The Ojibwa beat up the Naudoweg that time. The Ojibwa medicine man, Myeengun, predicted the Naudoweg arrival. All Naudoweg were drowned in their canoes.

Oh that Michipeshu, the big lynx with the horns. He's up north here. None of the underwater creatures were dangerous for the medicine men. You wouldn't say that they were dangerous or anything. But Michipeshu and the giant serpents were here to protect their tribe.

You see what happened there, when the Indians were invaded, it was

*the educated men (people who had fasted for spiritual power) who
asked those underwater creatures for help.*

The details of this story support the *Amikwa* identification pro-
posed for Myeengun. The early events in the Iroquois wars are easily
dated to the time between 1650 and 1662. In addition, Fred Pine's account of Myeengun's involvement in a battle near Agawa agrees with
Schoolcraft's account, including the detail of the Carp River being the
route that the Iroquois used to get to Lake Superior. According to
Schoolcraft, Myeengun also placed a group of pictographs at Carp
River to celebrate his victory.

From the evidence, we believe that Myeengun was an *Amikwa* leader from
northeastern Lake Huron, who was displaced to the Lake Superior
area, during the Iroquois wars of the late 17th century. At that time,
he battled the Iroquois on eastern Lake Superior, and made a commemorative pictograph panel during a ritual after the event.

We also know, from surviving historical records and native oral history,
that the last major battle between several united Ojibwa groups and the
marauding Iroquois took place in 1662 on eastern Lake Superior, just west
of Sault Ste. Marie. The French trader Perrot and the early Jesuit missionaries recorded the battle and commented on the skulls of the dead found on
Iroquois Point. The Agawa conflict must have taken place a year or two
before 1662, since the Iroquois Point battle was the last time the
Iroquois ever raided Lake Superior. In 1661, the displaced *Amikwa*
and Nipissing bands were reported temporarily living at Lake Nipigon,
on the north shore of Lake Superior. Myeengun was the *Amikwa* chief.

Shingwaukonce and Fred Pine both identified the group of canoes and
animal pictographs at Agawa as the work of Myeengun, The Wolf. From the
warfare mentioned in the oral history, the Myeengun panel appears to have
been painted between 1650 A.D. and 1662 A.D. It is a panel which shows
four, multiple occupant canoes, arranged vertically. A parallel series of
animal motifs includes a crane, a thunderbird or eagle, and a beaver.
Ojibwa elders have identified the animal motifs as totemic clan
symbols. The crane is one of the major totems for Sault Ste. Marie
area Ojibwa. Shingwaukonce, and his descendants in the Pine family,
have crane totems. The thunderbird motif is the same design drawn
by Mississagi band people from the north shore of Lake Huron. They
carry an eagle totem which is portrayed as a thunderbird.

The final totem on panel III is a beaver. The main totem of the

A diving beaver leads a row of canoes at the Little Missinaibi Lake site.

Amikwa, who lived at the mouth of the French River, refers to belief in a giant beaver ancestor. In fact, the tribal name *Amikwa* means 'Beaver People'. Today the residents of the French River and Pickerel River Indian Reserves on Georgian Bay still share the same beaver totems of their *Amikwa* forebearers. Some of the native people living there today could be descendants of Myeengun.

The Myeengun canoe panel at Agawa, with its ethnographic documentation and interpretation, provides a model for examining two other, similar groups of painted canoes. A diving beaver leads three canoes arranged vertically at the Little Missinaibi Lake pictograph site, located northeast of Lake Superior in Missinaibi Provincial Park. A similar panel occurs at the Ouisseau Rock site, located on the Ontario-Quebec border, where four canoes lined up vertically are led by two fish.

The use of animal totems to identify groups of Ojibwa was a practice featured in drawn messages. Frances Densmore, the noted anthropologist, collected a birchbark message from the Minnesota Ojibwa that helps us understand the Myeengun panel and identify the animals in front of the canoes as totem signs. For families travelling by canoe, the husband's totem was drawn in the bow of the canoe, the children's totem in the middle, and the wife's totem on the stern. The totemic concept behind these travel messages resembles the sorcery ritual rock art panels.

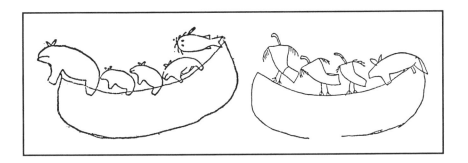

A birchbark drawing collected by Frances Densmore at the turn of the century shows Indian family members identified by their totem animals. The children have the same animal as their father in the bow. The mother's totem, in the stern, always differs.

Were There Two Medicine Men Named Shingwauk?

There may be more to learn from the Myeengun panel. During interviews with Fred Pine, he often spoke of his great-grandfather Shingwaukonce. There is no doubt about the accuracy of Fred Pine's stories. Many of the events mentioned, such as Shingwaukonce fighting with Brock in the War of 1812, can be cross-dated with written records. But some of the Pine family stories about Shingwaukonce fit less easily into the outline of the well documented, 19th century Shingwaukonce. For several years, we suspected there may have been another Shingwauk or Shingwaukonce who was an ancestor of the better known 'Pine'. We

*Shingwauk and his wife. The warrior and War of
1812 veteran wears his medal and trade silver ornaments.*

can not prove the following speculation, but it is based on enough information to be a very probable reconstruction. Was there another Pine family ancestor named Shingwauk who lived in the 17th century? And have some stories of his exploits survived? We think the answer is yes.

The first clue came from a story Fred Pine often told about Shingwauk meeting the first white people to land in North America.

Myeengun, Shingwauk, and the other educated men dreamed about people, that they never saw before, coming to Canada. White People. Sure enough, a few years after that, Shingwauk dreamed about a boat full of strange people. Ojibwa men went down the lakes until they hit the St. Lawrence River. At the mouth of the St. Lawrence River, they went to these big rocks. Shingwauk placed his men up on steep rocks. It's pretty well flat country down there with an occasional bluff. And that's where they signaled to each other. They watched for the ship. When the Indians knew it was near, Shingwauk performed a miracle.

He made the fog settle down so the boat could not land.

Shingwauk saw the boat before the fog settled down to the lake. And they could hear the people on the boat. They could hear the anchor dropping into the water. Boh-Kuhn-Djigun. Boh-Kuhn-Dji-Gay-wigis. 'An Anchor'. The anchor was thrown out and the Indians could hear the cogs letting down the chain. "Okay," Shingwauk said. "Let's go." That's when the Indians climbed on top of the boat and started banging the fellows on the head. I don't know how the Indians knew what was in those kegs. They had never seen guns or gunpowder before. Shingwauk said, "Load up all the kegs and throw the rest of it into the water." "Then these strangers will not be able to use their guns," he explained to the Ojibwa warriors. The Indians leaders knew the Europeans had some kind of a weapon that could be used to take over the land.

That time the white men did not land. More than half were killed. The Ojibwa leaders said, "Go back." Well, the people in the boat could not understand the Indian language, but they understood the warning. So the white people's ship went back across the ocean. But the medicine man predicted their return. "This ocean is a big lake," he said. "It'll take them two years to return. We must prepare." And that boat just left. But another boat landed on the St. Lawrence a few years later.

During a visit to Agawa in the mid-1980s, Fred Pine spoke about Shingwauk painting some pictographs at Agawa during the Iroquois wars. The Iroquois wars took place in the middle to late 17th century. When asked about the paintings, Fred Pine stated:

Shingwauk made some of the paintings at Agawa. What Shingwauk was scared of was the Iroquois coming up into Ojibwa country on Lake Superior. The Iroquois did not have the furs that we have here. You see, we have the best climate in Canada, in Ontario, for good furs. There's too much salt water to make perfect fur in Quebec. It's surrounded by salt water. Where the Iroquois came from, they didn't have the country for fur animals.

So the Iroquois knew the fur was better here. They said, "We'll go over to Lake Superior and take that country over. But that didn't happen. The Ojibwa knocked the Iroquois out of this area. That's when the Ojibwa medicine men made the markings on the rock.

Shingwauk made the markings for the other Ojibwa headmen. The big leaders of the Ojibwa. They were coming along the shore looking for a place where they would see the markings (pictographs). That's the reason Shingwauk put that mark on the rock. It's just like writing a letter to somebody. When the other Ojibwa medicine men came by Agawa, they would see the paintings. That's why Shingwauk did that. The Iroquois couldn't understand it. The Iroquois have different signs too. But the Iroquois are not explorers like the Ojibwa.

Shingwauk went up to Agawa with the other Ojibwa tribes. They knew the Iroquois were going to come and attack Lake Superior. There was no way the Ojibwa could stop the Iroquois. The Iroquois went everywhere. They came through Chicago and all through the Great Lakes.

There is a short-cut canoe route across the upper peninsula of Michigan from north of St. Ignace to Whitefish Bay on Lake Superior. The Iroquois crossed there to sneak around the Ojibwa villages at the Soo. They went up the Carp River, Wapagish Zibi. That's the route from Lake Michigan, up the Wapagish Zibi quite a distance. That is nearly all flat country. The Carp River hits Trout Lake. They went through the lakes in the upper peninsula to come out near Whitefish Bay. Some of that is swamp country. All flat.

The Iroquois knew about that route and they came over to Lake Superior. My people could have stopped them at the Soo, but the Iroquois went around behind to get in Lake Superior. The Iroquois got here, but they didn't stay very long because old Shingwauk put the jinx on them.

Shingwauk was a powerful medicine man. He knew somebody was coming to Lake Superior. He had a dream (vision) and he saw the Iroquois canoes. The south star appeared to him. There's something about Shawanung, 'The South Star' that means fear. There is a bad thing about the south. The South Star causes trouble. Nothing rises in the south. Not the sun, the moon, or the stars.

The medicine man said, "There's something bad coming from the south." Sure enough, that is where the Iroquois came from when they invaded the Ojibwa. South. They all came from the south.

This story is hard to translate. When the Iroquois came into this area, the Ojibwa asked for help across Lake Superior. The Ojibwa did not have radios. How did they get the message from one side of the lake to *the other? Well you know what? They had that medicine man fly over there.*

He flew over there, across Lake Superior. It would not take very long to get over to the south shore. The medicine man could use any fast bird he could get hold of. He even used that Nah-Noh-Kah-Say. It will fly across the ocean. That's the hummingbird. He was sent for messages.

Oh, they won. My people won. Well, at Agawa, that's where the old chiefs met. So Shingwauk said, "When the Iroquois come in, I'll perform a fog on them." He made a heavy fog. Shingwauk opened up the fog. He lifted up the fog so he could see a long ways. That's what he did. He fogged up all of Lake Superior. Shingwauk made a large fire, and his people danced around the fire and put tobacco in it. Then he performed the miracle. He had the power to affect the atmosphere and lift the fog.

When the Ojibwa tribes went out, they went and met the Iroquois out on the lake. They never landed. The Iroquois never landed here on the north shore of Lake Superior. Shingwauk told the warriors to watch for the Iroquois. He placed his men on top of cliffs around the lake to watch. They covered themselves with brush like hay. And put hay all over the ground so they could not be seen. It was a camouflage.

Then the Ojibwa wrapped their paddles with beaver hides to soften the sounds. Some kind of a hide. They didn't make any noise with the canoes. The Ojibwa warriors went in there just as quiet as could be. And they ran the Iroquois out. In the big battle, the Ojibwa got the jump on the enemy. They grabbed them and killed the Iroquois with wooden clubs. There were no guns in those days.

The Iroquois never landed here. Well, the Ojibwa had a bunch of troops up the river too. There's some caves up here in Agawa. Many people were hidden up there.

Caves are a good hideout for the Indians. The Iroquois didn't know anything about rapids. There's no rough water in Quebec where the Iroquois lived on the St. Lawrence River.

These Ojibwa Indians here could portage rapids. They could take their canoes up rivers, anywhere. I did that myself. I used poles on the Montreal River to go up. Get the canoe this way and push it up there. You use it for going down with a big load. We checked the canoe so it

*Huge Ojibwa caones capable of holding
many individuals were still being built at the Soo less
than a century ago.*

won't hit the rock. If we saw rocks ahead of us, we would stop the canoe
with the pole.

After that, Shingwauk and the other powerful headmen painted those
markings on the rock at Agawa. You see, those were a warning.

Shingwauk knew everything. He was the fellow that took the Lake
Superior Ojibwa down to the St. Lawrence when the first white man's
boats landed in North America. All of the headmen gathered at Soo,
Michigan. They had big birchbark canoes thirty feet long.

Understanding The Michipeshu Panel

For many years, the central *Michipeshu* panel was one of a handful of Ojibwa rock art panels which had been explained by medicine men.

In the upper Great Lakes area of Michigan and Ontario, one of the more famous 19th century native American leaders was an Ojibwa named Shingwaukonce or 'Little White Pine'. This shaman, political leader, and warrior was born in 1773 and lived until 1854. Shingwaukonce's life spanned several pivotal events in the destiny of the Ojibwa, including the War of 1812, Indian uprisings, and the beginning of the treaty and reservation periods. Shingwaukonce participated in these events as a leader and astute politician.

There are two sources available to reconstruct Shingwaukonce's life. The first involves the documents of the many travellers, Indian agents, treaty conveners, and missionaries who came in contact with Shingwaukonce. Also, the Indian agent Henry Schoolcraft provides extensive political and ethnographic documentation of Shingwaukonce. The second major source for understanding Shingwaukonce comes through the oral history preserved by his descendants.

Shingwaukonce was a complex individual. His mother, *Ogima-Kwae* or 'Woman Chief', gave birth to Shingwaukonce at Grand Island, Michigan. Shingwaukonce's father was a French trader named Lavoine Bart. Although Shingwaukonce had part Euro-Canadian ancestory, he was clearly raised as an Ojibwa Indian. He spoke only Ojibwa. From his mother, Shingwaukonce inherited the crane totem, which subsequently appeared on several treaties signed by him or his sons; although on the treaty of 1820, Shingwaukonce signed his name as Lavoine Bart.

The earliest reference to Shingwaukonce comes from a trader's journal, dated February 3, 1791, when he arrived at the upper Michigan settlement of Michilimackinac. He is referred to as 'Chincoake, chief of the Saulteaux'. In June 1791, Shingwaukonce returned to Michilimackinac with "his band". Shingwaukonce was recognized, at an early age, as a leader. He served as chief of the Saulteaux as early as the age of 18. Military records and native oral history show that Shingwauk was a veteran of the War Of 1812. He fought with Brock near Niagara Falls. Later in his life, Shingwauk signed the 1850 Robinson-Huron treaty, and lead a revolt against the copper miners at Mamainse on Lake Superior.

Without the guidance offered by his descendants, Fred Pine and Dan Pine, the use of Shingwauk's name is confusing. Historical documents refer to the great leader as *Shingwauk, Shingwaukonce*, 'The Pine', *Chingwauk* and *Chincoake*. The root of this family name is correctly translated as 'White Pine'. Just as Fred Pine's surname is shortened to 'Pine', so was Shingwauk called 'The Pine'. *Shingwauk, Chingwauk,* and *Chingoake* are various spellings of the same Ojibwa word. Spellings vary because the Ojibwa Indian language does not have a standardized system of spelling.

Fred Pine and Dan Pine explained how the various uses of Shingwauk (The White Pine) and Shingwaukonce (The Little White Pine) referred to the same person; and the use of these terms has shamanic connotations. A shaman gains power from the sun; and the sun's position in the sky affects the strength of this cosmic power. Shingwauk was a *Wabeno* shaman. A *Wabeno* specialized in the regulation of the natural order on earth, fertility, and the reincarnation of souls by studying the stars, the moon and the sun. Shingwauk's personal name was *Sah-Kah-Odjew-Wahg-Sah* or 'Sun Rising Over The Mountain'. This shamanic name conveys the power of the moment of sunrise to a person.

Dan Pine continues to observe the ancient Ojibwa rituals which offer respect to the great powers in nature. He carefully explained our relationship to the sun.

Respect everything in nature. Like the sun. Rise with the sun. Work with the sun. Work like the sun works. The sun will walk with you

A pictograph from Scotia Lake shows a
shaman literally enlightened, or filled with the light of the
sun.

(provide protective powers). The sun will repect you. Take care of
you. Give you light.

In the secret shamanic usage, you would properly refer to this
medicine man as *Sah-Kah-Odjew-Wahg-Sah* meaning the hours
between sunrise and noon. The name Shingwauk or 'White Pine'
conveys the image of the most powerful tree reaching into the
heavens. Because of a white pine's longevity, this tree symbolized
immortality. Of all the trees along the northern Great Lakes, the pine
ascended the greatest distance into the sky world.

Dan Pine understands the meaning of the white pine.

The white pine was the boss (chief) of all trees in co-operation with the sun and the moon. Some other trees wanted to be bigger. Many of the small trees have a lot of power. If they became bigger, the small trees would harm the world. The white pine could control its own power.

These beliefs formed the background to Shingwauk's name. He would be called Shingwauk from noon to early evening, and Shingwaukonce from early evening to sunset indicates the sun's waning power. A complicated set of beliefs and ritualistic observances are built into these names. In this guide book, we use the names Shingwauk and Shingwaukonce interchangeably as do many modern native speakers.

Shingwaukonce was a grand shaman of the Lake Superior Ojibwa. He fasted for spiritual development for ten days at a time on ten separate occasions. Among the stoic Ojibwa, four days served as the usual length of a fast. Tales of Shingwaukonce's vision quests were noted with awe by 19th century observers such as the German traveller Kohl. These stories can also be collected today from Shingwauk's living descendants. Some of Shingwaukonce's fasts ended with rituals that included the creation of pictographs. Two rock art panels at Agawa are attributed to Shingwaukonce, and a third pictograph panel has been interpreted by Shingwaukonce and by his living descendants.

Shingwaukonce's exploits remain alive in the oral history of the Garden River Ojibwa. The following stories, told by Fred Pine, help us appreciate this man and his powers.

You see this man, Shingwaukonce, was a medicine man. He was one of the strongest medicine men on the north shore. All the Ojibwa Indians were originally from Lake Superior. That's what they call Dji-Gwaybs-Chi-Kih-May. 'The Big Ojibwa Lake'.

The old chief, Shingwaukonce, was my (great) grandfather. He controlled everything. They put him in as honorary chief. He could see all of the Ojibwa people around Lake Superior. So when the trouble started when the white men first moved in, some (Ojibwa) moved south. He fought the copper miners.

Shingwaukonce was hired to contact Indians because he had the power. He could fly over someplace. And you know, he could go any place by turning himself into a bird.

Oh my, I could tell stories about Shingwaukonce from now until next July. I picked this knowledge up when I was young. The woman that raised me was one of Shingwauk's granddaughters. She said old Shingwauk used to lock himself up in a loft. He had a home partitioned off. I know the place. I've been in it. The house is lived in yet. A fellow bought that house and moved it onto Squirrel Island.

The house is partitioned off where the stairway is. Shingwaukonce stayed behind the partition. He locked the doors up. He just came out sometimes. Some days they didn't know where he was. He's gone. But his body was still there. A long journey. California. Nothing could stop that man.

It's kind of dangerous. When somebody like that leaves their body. You can't disturb the body that's there. Oh, Shingwaukonce's family knew that he'd go in that room there to turn into a soul.

Dan Pine also remembers many stories about his grandfather.

My grandfather fasted ten times to receive ten gifts. These medals I hold belonged to Shingwauk. He got them for fighting in the War Of 1812. A white pine will never die. Shingwauk could turn into anything. Any animal. He wore buckskins full of bullet holes from the war; but the bullets would not penetrate his skin. He was protected.

Lightening can not be killed. Lightening was one of Shingwauk's gifts. Shingwauk was a quickening spirit. Like smoke. Nothing could be hidden from him.

One time the Indians had a gathering. Two guys were sent from out west to kill Shingwauk. At that time, this area (eastern Lake Superior) was the most powerful place. Here on this central part of the island (earth). When the men tried to kill Shingwauk, he dropped his medicine bag intentionally. Shingwauk exposed his back so they could knife him. The strangers raised their hands, but the knives dropped to the ground. Shingwauk kept picking up his pouch. Shingwauk told them to pick up their knives and put them away. The men took off after this encounter with Shingwauk's power.

The following story indicates Shingwaukonce's humor which Fred Pine definitely inherited.

Old Shingwauk is coming back (from the dead). Oh yeah, he's just gone for repairs. Well I was told that. He's coming back. I believe that too.

You know what the priest once said to Shingwaukonce? "Do you believe in the soul, Mr. Shingwauk?" Shingwaukonce replied, "you're talking to a soul right now." What could the priest say? Shingwaukonce was telling the truth. He could take off. He could make himself into a bird, snake, anything. He was the soul.

With a background as a supreme shaman, Shingwauk made use of the Agawa site. Not suprisingly, local Ojibwa elders indicated that Shingwauk produced the main *Michipeshu* panel. Unlike the Myeengun War Party panel and the Horse and Rider panel, where the shaman artists were clearly identified, the association between Shingwauk and the *Michipeshu* group has been difficult to fully document.

Apparently, Shingwauk went to Agawa to gather fresh power on a vision quest. He called forth *Michipeshu*, the guardian spirit of the underworld and minerals, especially copper. Shingwauk completed his fast, finished rituals which included rock art, and then lead his warriors in a revolt against the copper miners at Mamainse.

Secrets Of The Horse
And Rider Panel

After the main *Michipeshu* panel, the horse and rider group of pictographs raises the most questions from visitors to the site. The presence of a horse makes the art a little less foreign to those not familiar with native culture and its symbolism. Most people expect to learn a story from the interrelated pictographs on this panel.

According to his descendants, Shingwaukonce not only knew many details about the origins of certain pictographs at Agawa, but he actually painted some of the panels including the horse and rider group.

Ojibwa elders have indicated that Shingwaukonce painted the large *Michipeshu*, underwater creature panel, as well as the Agawa horse and rider panel. Both of these panels contain pictographic elements that are consistent with Shingwaukonce's life and shamanic deeds.

The horse and rider panel was completed after a ten day fast associated with a ritual duel between Shingwaukonce and a rival shaman over the spiritual leadership of the Lake Superior Ojibwa. Many pictographic clues within the panel relate to Shingwauk's powers.

Several centuries ago, the Ojibwa Indians developed a religious movement named the *Midewewin* or 'Grand Medicine Society'. This religion is devoted to healing and the developement of personal spiritual powers. The *Midewewin* has a complex series of ceremonies, levels of initiation, and special religious structures.

We know that Shingwaukonce reached the highest level of the *Midewewin*, the fourth degree. According to the elders interviewed,

A midewewin lodge from northern Lake Superior. Shingwauk was a mide healer as well as a specialist in other forms of Indian shamanism.

pictographic references to this achievement appear within the horse and rider panel at Agawa. The first is the presence of the characteristic *Mide* cross.

In the *Midewewin* ceremonial lodges, posts are erected with an increasing number of posts for each degree level, until the fourth degree is reached. Posts from the first three levels are painted vertical logs, but the fourth level post contains a cross-piece. Several Ojibwa birch bark scrolls from Minnesota also show the *Mide* cross on third and fourth degree levels. Native elders have explained how this symbol refers to four guardian spirits. This *Mide* cross symbol predates European influence. Traditionalist Indian religious leaders today remember Shingwaukonce as a fourth degree *Midewewin* leader; and the presence of the fourth degree cross in the dream panel refers to this achievement.

Apparently, cross-poles also had ritual functions for outside of the *Midewewin* context. For example, the Spanish River Indians on Lake Huron hung ribbons and tobacco on cross-poles as offerings to the spirits.

The four painted spheres on the Agawa horse and rider panel are rare motifs in Algonkian rock art, but they appear more commonly on mide scrolls. These spheres were not interpreted by the tribal elders we interviewed. However, a thorough analysis of *Midewewin* prayer scrolls from Minnesota revealed numerous examples of circles or spheres, which *Mide* priests identified as "songs and prayers," or "centers of spiritual activity." One scroll has four spheres as part of a *Mide* lodge entrance ritual. This is the closest example to the four spheres found below the horse and rider at Agawa.

The insect in front of the horse is a louse according to Shingwaukonce's descendants. A legend tells how Shingwaukonce transformed himself into a louse in order to ride a raven into the spirit world.

Fred Pine provided a somewhat cryptic account about horses after viewing the horse and rider panel.

Medicine men changed what they did with the horse by transplanting and crossbreeding them so horses wouldn't have horns. They shaped the horse who had the horns. They thought it was the devil. So when you see a horse, don't go there. Drive by.

Schoolcraft presented a story about the horse and rider panel which is neither consistent with the art on the panel, nor the native oral history. The historical details recorded by Schoolcraft for the Myeen-gun canoe panel are accurate, and Schoolcraft appears to have presented that story as related by Shingwaukonce. But, Schoolcraft's analysis of the horse and rider panel, which interprets the three spheres as "three suns under a sky and a rainbow," may be conjecture on his part. Schoolcraft's observations and interpretations of Ojibwa culture are generally excellent, although he did exaggerate his knowledge on occasion. This interpretation of the horse and rider panel is not consistent with the oral history supplied by local Ojibwa elders or with Algonkian pictography in general.

*The horse and rider is much
larger than most paintings.*

Lake Superior Provincial Park Indian History

In the early 1970's, archaeologists made site surveys of Lake Superior Provincial Park. Several dozen archaeological sites were discovered including Indian villages and campsites, burial grounds, three rock art sites, the mysterious puckasaw pits on cobble beaches, a Hudson's Bay Company fur trade post site, and several Indian sacred sites. Excavations uncovered artifacts representing over three thousand years of Indian settlement.

In the historical era, the present land within Lake Superior Provincial Park was used by two Indian bands. The north end of the park, north of Gamitagama and Mijinemungshing Lakes, was the ancestral trapping territory of a family from the Michipicoten band. The area from Gargantua south to Agawa was the coastline portion of the Agawa band's territory. The Agawa band lived in the Agawa Bay settlements until the turn of the century when epidemics greatly reduced the population. The surviving families moved to the Batchewana Bay area.

William Schelling's was the last Hudson'sBay Company trader at Agawa Bay. His daughter grew up at the Agawa fur post and Indian village. Her reminiscences tell a tragic story.

> Came the "famine winter" of 1879. There was no
> game in the bush, and the fish, packed in pork
> barrels, all rotted. The Indians ate chipmunks and

squirrels, and the dogs all died. The weather was unusually severe and the ice used to move out into the lake until nothing but clear water could be seen, and then would drift back and pile up on the beach. It was then the waters of the Agawa backed and threatened the post.

According to custom the Indians used to take the bones and the heads of the bear they killed out to Agawa Rock and "decorate them". Food became so scarce that these bones were all taken from the island, and boiled with fungus, bear grease and small potatoes that had been thrown away, for food. Many of the Indians died. William Schelling left for Michipicoten for supplies, but on the return trip was jammed in the ice, and the food had to be packed back to the post. It was distributed to the Indians, and all ate so much that they became sick. The cemetery grew that winter.

The hard times described at the Agawa Indian village and Hudson'sBay Company outpost document the end of Indian life on a part of Lake Superior settled for thousands of years. In 1973, a knowledgable eldernamed Angus Kapkapshe pointed out the cemetery at Agawa Bay where the famine victims lay buried.

Indian spirit houses mark past settlements across northern Ontario.

Other Rock Art Sites
On Lake Superior

Very few pictograph sites have been discovered on Lake Superior. While the Agawa Rock site is the most famous, a few more sites which contribute to an understanding of Ojibwa art. Within Lake Superior Provincial Park, two more sites have been recorded. Important pictograph sites are located on the coast near the town of Schreiber and near the mouth of the Nipigon River. More small sites remain hidden along the hundreds of miles of rocky Lake Superior shore.

One small site, named the Vandalized Pictograph site, is located south of Agawa Rock. Discovered in the early 1970's, it has a few linear abstract motifs on one panel. Another small rock art site in Lake Superior Provincial Park was observed near Gargantua by the noted outdoor author Wayland Drew and Gwen Drew. A canoe and some vertical lines are painted on that cliff. A report of pictographs near the Agawa Falls on the Agawa River awaits confirmation.

Mike O'Connor and his famous husky Winston recently discovered a single painting of a stick figure style person in an isolated section of Puckasaw National park. Other sites west of the Puckasaw have not been seen since the days of the voyageurs. But local place names, such as Les Petits Ecrits or 'The Little Writings', preserve their memory.

The next recorded rock art on Lake Superior is found inside a small rock shelter near Schreiber, Ontario. The rock art at this site is very different than the Agawa site. Human figures are much more common. The location of the Schreiber site is kept undisclosed to help protect the pictographs.

The much more extensive Nipigon Bay site has been studied since the turn of the century. Access to the Nipigon site is made by boat or canoe. Visitors will find a huge cliff with a series of painted dots, canoes, and unusual abstract designs.

During his work with Henry Schoolcraft, Shingwauk reported a pictograph site on the south shore of Lake Superior. It was associated with the war chief Myeengun and a crossing of Lake Superior. Selwyn Dewdney searched for the south shore site without success. The site may have been weathered away because of soft sandstone cliffs. However, some Chippewa Indians from the Marquette area indicated that the site has been seen within recent memory. A separate small rock art site has been found on an island near Marquette.

The Vandalized pictograph site is located near Agawa Rock. A few lines are painted in a small area.

About The Authors

Thor Conway is an archaeologist/anthropologist who has worked in the upper Great Lakes area for seventeen years. He has discovered numerous prehistoric and historic Indian sites, fur posts, rock art sites, and stone tool workshops across northeastern Ontario from Manitoulin Island and Sault Ste Marie to Temagami and Moose Factory Island. In addition to excavating sites, he works extensively with tribal elders recording native folklore and oral history. Thor Conway has interviewed and studied with the last Ojibwa shamans, medicine men and medicine women.

Thor Conway was born an archaeologist, and he loves to share with the public the fascinating stories revealed through excavations at sites and conversations with tribal elders. He leads tours to sites in Ontario and California, conducts digs open to volunteers, and writes popular books and articles about native American heritage.

Julie Matey Conway is an artist who records her impressions of the

natural world with watercolor paintings. Her work has been shown in the United States and Canada. In addition to her personal artwork, she does scientific illustrations and studies rock art.

Thor and Julie Conway live near Echo Bay, Ontario where they share their love of nature with their two daughters.

Learning More About Rock Art & Indian Culture

The following sources will lead to a greater understanding of native culture and rock art. If you have any questions, feel free to write to us.

Heritage Discoveries Publications   Heritage Discoveries publishes several books about rock art, the secrets of Indian medicine men, archaeology, Indian folklore, and oral history. We also offer tours to rock art and other archaeological sites.

To receive notices about our publications and tours, or to order additional copies of this book, send your name and address to : **Heritage Discoveries**, P.O. Box 269, Echo Bay, Ontario, Canada POSICO; or P.O. Box 916, Sault Ste Marie, Michigan, U.S.A.   49783.

American Rock Art Research Associates (ARARA) is an excellent source of information about rock art sites, current research, publications, and field trips in the United States and Canada. The newsletter is filled with articles and book reviews. The yearly journal, American ndian Rock Art, contains research papers from the annual meetings. Write: ARARA, P.O. Box 65, San Miguel, California   93451.

UCLA Rock Art Archive has an extensive publication series ranging from specific site reports to regional studies and popular books. Write: Rock Art Archive, 68 Kinsey Hall, UCLA, Los Angeles. California 90024.

Table 1: Agawa Pictograph Site Motifs

---

(29) ANIMAL MOTIFS

1 Beaver (#12)	2 Mammals (#114 & #115)
1 Shore bird (#10)	1 Turtle with trail (#112)
1 Moose (#15)	3 Caribou (#5, #100 & #101)
2 Fish (#1 & #107)	1 Horse & rider (#79)
1 Insect (louse) (#80)	2 Bears (#95 & #96)
2 Thunderbirds (#4 & #11)	1 Horned general mammal (#94)
3 Michipeshus (#66, #104, & #109)	1 Horned creature with legs (#2)
5 Bear tracks (#16, #17, #21, #42 & #44)	2 Snakes (#54 & #55)

---

(2) ANTHROPOMORPHS

2 People in profile holding drums (#102 & #103)

---

(15) CANOE MOTIFS

1 Five occupant canoe (#3)	1 Deep five person canoe (#56)
3 Five occupant canoes (#6 to #8)	1 Eight occupant canoe (#9)
1 Two occupant canoe (#108)	1 Two occupant canoe (#117)
1 Small two occupant canoe (#82)	1 Two occupant canoe (#91)
1 Canoe with person and paddle (#99)	1 Two occupant canoe (#105)

1 Two occupant canoe with paddles (#13)

1 Large, incompletely preserved canoe (#14)

1 Large canoe with three shaped occupants (#74)

---

(58) ABSTRACT MOTIFS

1 Short oblique line (#98)	1 Long oblique line (#43)
1 Vertical line (#83)	3 Tallys (#18 to #20)
1 Triangle with tail (#73)	3 Tallys (#26 to #28)
4 Spheres (#75 to #78)	3 Tallys (#29 to #31)
1 Long cross (#81)	3 Tallys (#45 to #47)

3 Long tallys (#34 to #36)

3 Oblique tallys (#38 to #40)

5 Horizontal lines (#86 to #90)

1 Tally (#24)

1 Ochre wash (#71)

1 Small circle (#37)

2 Vertical lines (#64 & #65)

2 Large enclosing circles (#84 & #85)

1 Grouped finger drags joined at the base (#41)

2 Daubs (#110 & #113)

1 Tally (#23)

3 Finger drags (#48 to #50)

3 Finger drags (#51 to #53)

3 Finger drags (#58 to #60)

3 Finger drags (#61 to #63)

3 Finger drags (#68 to #70)

(13) FAINT MOTIFS

13 faint   (#22, #25, #32, #33, #57, #67, #72, #92, #93, #97, #106, #111 & #116)

Individual Paintings On Each Panel

Panel I = #1 to #4

Panel III = #6 to #12

Panel V = #14

Panel VII-A= #16 to #20

Panel VII-C = #21 to #32

Panel VII-E = #42 to #50

Panel IX   = #73 & #74

Panel XI   = #91 to #93

Panel XIII = #99 to #101

Panel XV   = #104 & #105

Panel XVII = #112 & #113

Panel II = #5

Panel IV = #13

Panel VI = #15

Panel VII-B= #33 to #40

Panel VII-D= #41

Panel VIII = #51 to #72

Panel X = #75 to #90

Panel XII = #94 to #98

Panel XIV = #102 & #103

Panel XVI = #106 to #111

Panel XVIII = #114 to #117